To Dorr. —

I SURVIVED
THE
KILLINGFIELDS

Sam Ung

5/12/11

The true life story of a Cambodian refugee

SENG KOK UNG

If you enjoy the book please let us know by emailing us at either
sam-ung@live.com
or thomas_mcelroy@hotmail.com

we can also be reached at our facebook pages which is
Seng Ung http://www.facebook.com/#!/profile.php?id=100001544338410
or Thomas McElroy http://www.facebook.com/#!/profile.php?id=1405465798

INTRODUCTION

Torture, starvation, brutal and arbitrary executions, brainwashed children spying on parents. These are only some of the horror Cambodians had to go through under the brutal Khmer Rouge regime. During their time in power selected groups of people simply "disappeared". Intellectuals, people who wore glasses, doctors, and lawyers were the first to be executed. They wanted no one around who may have the potential to undermine their plans for the new Cambodia.

The Khmer Rouge took over the country and carried out a radical program that isolated the country from "outside sources" closing schools, hospitals and factories. They abolished banking, finance and currency, outlawed all religions and moved city dwellers out to the countryside where people were literally worked to death. Millions of people died through executions, work exhaustion, illness and starvation.

Family relationships not sanctioned by the state were banned. Family members could be put to death for even talking with each other. The leadership of villages even had the power over who was able to get married and to whom they would be married to.

This is the backdrop of what my life was like for four long years. Amazingly, through it all, most of my family members stayed close to each other. Some of the family members died from starvation and several members were executed. To this day their bodies have never been located.

In the pages that follow is my journey through the hellish nightmare of the Khmer Rouge, to Thailand and eventually to the United States where I literally transformed myself into the quintessential American success story.

My mother and grandmother were both very serious Buddhists. Whenever they came across a farmer who was selling caged birds, they would buy the whole cage, say a Buddhist prayer and set the birds free so the birds would stay together. They prayed that their family would be like the birds and remain together. But it never came true because we have family all over the world now. This is the story of our family's flight.

—*Sam Ung*

ACKNOWLEDGMENTS

This book is dedicated to the memory of my mother and father and to the family members that I lost during the Khmer Rouge's takeover of Cambodia.

To my brothers (Tong Meng, Kheang, Kheng, Heng, and Chai) and sister (Say Ky), who survived this horrible ordeal: I am thankful to you that we are all still close and a family. Our parents' dream was to have us remain close, and we worked very hard during those years to live up to their hopes for us.

To all my nieces and nephews: This book will help you understand what your older family members endured, how it affected their lives and what eventually became of us once we reached the United States.

To my children, Dawn, Diane and Darlene, my son-in-law Damon; and my grandchildren, Devin and Derin: I wrote this book to help exorcise the horrors of my past, which I have never talked about with you. The stories in this book will allow you to understand better what our family has endured—and why we value each other so much now.

And, of course, to my wife of thirty years, Kim Ung: None of this would have been possible without you. You have been a source of strength and determination in our lives and raised our children so they could blossom. When we came to this country from a Thai refugee camp so many years ago, we started with literally nothing except each other. Thanks to our partnership, we persevered to become a true American success story.

Finally, to Thomas McElroy: Thank you for helping me write my memoir.

MY FAMILY

My name is Seng Kok Ung, but people call me Sam. I am 56 years old and for the last 30 years, since my wife and I escaped from Cambodia, we have lived in Seattle, Washington. I own a Cambodian restaurant called Phnom Penh Noodle House in the International District and run a catering business as well. I have been blessed with three lovely daughters and two wonderful grandchildren. I am very proud to be a citizen of the United States. The day I became a citizen was one of the best days of my life. As a child, I had never dreamt that my life would take me from my native country of Cambodia across an ocean to America. But as a child I had also never imagined that something like the Khmer Rouge occupation could ever exist. This is the story of my life during the Khmer Rouge takeover of Cambodia, my escape to America, and how I built a life here, started a family, and made this new place my home.

Let us start at the beginning.

I was born February 28, 1955, in Battambang. It's Cambodia's second largest city, and is located in the northwestern part of the country near Thailand, in a province nick-named the rice bowl of Cambodia because of its ability to produce three rice crops a year. I was the fifth of nine children born to my mother, Meng Vouch, and my father, Chan Kao.

My father was born in the city of Jieyang in Canton Province, China in 1923. He fled to Cambodia in 1937 at the age of 14 to avoid being conscripted into the Chinese Army. Many of his friends had been sent off to fight in the Sino-Japanese War (July 7, 1937-September 9, 1945) and he wanted nothing to do it. He packed his bag with some food, said goodbye to his family members, wished them all good luck and departed.

Traveling with friends, my father's little group walked and hitched rides to Shenzhen (about 643 kilometers) then took a boat across the South China Sea landing somewhere in Vietnam. From there the band of friends walked into Cambodia. My father never told me how long the trip took so I can only imagine it must have taken at least several month's or longer to travel that distance. They left home with nothing and once the food ran out they turned to begging for the rest of the trip. All they had were the clothes they were wearing. Their cloth pants and shirts were dirty, torn and tattered. The soles of their shoes were worn thin with maybe a toe or two sticking out, unwashed expect for stopping to bathe in local streams. They must have been quite a disheveled looking group.

My father considered himself fortunate, for he found work right away as a farm laborer. He worked from morning to night carrying dirt to various farms in the area. He didn't have a place to live yet so he took up residence in a Buddhist temple. The monks were kind, fed him every day and in return for the work he did, they allowed him to stay at the monastery. My father lived at the there for four years before moving to Battambang, where he started his noodle-cart business.

My mother was born in 1927 in the city of Kampong Chhnang in Cambodia. Of Chinese-Vietnamese descent, she was the youngest of four sisters and two brothers. My grandfather owned a boat, and he traveled with it up and down the Mekong River, where he traded fruits, vegetables and wares like pots and pans with the Vietnamese and like any good businessman supplied anything his clients asked for. This made him a wealthy man and as a result, my mother was well educated and learned to read and write Thai, Vietnamese, Cambodian, and French as well as three different Chinese dialects which were TeoChew, Fukin, and Cantonese.

Since my maternal grandfather was often gone on business in Vietnam, he ended up keeping a mistress (whom he could visit regularly through his trading business). When my grandmother found out about the mistress, she packed up their belongings and moved with her female children to Battambang. The women's relatively comfortable life came to an abrupt end and for a time were forced to live in a grain storage shed while they figured out how to make their own living. They came up with a recipe for rice candy and took the sweets to sell at the Battambang market. My mother talked often about these times as being extremely hard on her sisters and mother. There was often very little to eat or drink and things like getting a hot bath were looked upon as something special and quite frankly did not happen that often. My mother was 14 years old when this happened and she always talked about how the experience shaped her life by forcing her to become self-sufficient. She could no longer take things for granted and began to realize how quickly things can go from good to bad. Fate, it seems, was working on my mother's behalf because soon her life was to take another turn.

While pushing his noodle cart around Battambang my father saw my grandmother and mother. The chance meeting occurred at the public market as they sat patiently on the street selling their neatly wrapped rice candies. He was immediately struck with my mother's looks and because of that felt compelled to strike up a conversation with my grandmother. My grandmother was so impressed with him that she decided my mother would marry him. It was her way of gaining a son-in-law which would bring more stability to their little clan of women and would also offer protection for them. Their need for protection was one of my grandmother's main concerns as the Japanese were occupying Cambodia. Making matters worse were rumours of stories about the cruelty of the soldiers towards local women.

My father was 21 and my mother was 17 when they married in 1942. Things were extremely difficult during their early years of marriage. Thing were so hard when they married that they only had potato sacks as clothes. Their first home was in a swampy area of the city filled with mosquitoes and swamp grass. I do not know why this place was chosen as an area to build in. Maybe the land was cheap or free? The floor of the shack was fashioned from old boards, the walls from branches tied together with grasses bound together like rope. Grass and mud were then compacted together to fashion walls to keep wind and rain out. Being built in a swamp the hut had to be off of the ground several inches so they built stairs up to the front door. Finishing off the place was a roof out of elephant grass.

While living in the mud hut the two of them would ready the cart daily by stopping by the public market to pick up groceries for that day's soup base making then find a spot to set up shop. They tried to be consistent about where they set up so their growing clientele could find them. Along with working to cultivate the business their family started to grow as well. Within a year of getting married, my mother gave birth to their first son, Tong Meng. A second son, Kok Meng, was born in 1943. Kok Kheang, their third son, was born in 1948; Say Ky, their first daughter, was born in 1950. Kok Kheng was born in 1952. I was their fifth son and was born in 1955. Kok Heng their sixth son was born in 1958. Kok Chhay, son number seven born in 1964. Lastly, the second daughter, Say Kim, arrived in 1967.

My Mother and Father in 1965

In 1964, after several years of successfully running their noodle-cart business, my parents had saved enough money to open a café in the public market in Battambang. They kept the same noodle soup recipe but added congee and desserts. They named the restaurant Ung Hong Lee, which means "The Ung family will prosper." The restaurant was open 24 hours a day, seven days a week with a dozen employees working two twelve hour shifts with no days off. My parents worked incredibly hard to make the café a success and within two years they were able to buy the seafood restaurant next door. This marked the café's beginning as a full-fledged restaurant. In no time, lines snaked out the door all day long. They cooked 100 pounds of rice every day, which represents the large quantity of people they served food to daily.

My brothers and sister in 1965
Top row: Say Ky, Kok Kheang, Kok Meng, Tong Meng
Bottom row: Kok Heng, Seng Kok (me) Kok Chai, Kok Kheng

When I was little, I loved watching the rapid-fire movements of the cooks as they grabbed woks off the flame, dumped the food on the plate, and returned the woks back on the stove in one continuous motion. Moving so quickly and in harmony with each other it looked like a magical dance.

Observing these men is the moment I realized I wanted to perform that dance and create magic in my own kitchen someday.

My father was becoming an increasingly prominent and important member of the community. He regularly sent money back to his mother and siblings in China, and even managed to bring two of his brothers to Cambodia, where he helped them start their own businesses. Actively involved in the local Chinese community he served as the president of the TeoChew Association for 20 years. In addition, he served as the president of the Chinese cemetery and generously spent his own money on caskets and plots for people without family to arrange burial rites. He also was a member of the Chinese school board. Everyone in the community knew him and respected him for his generosity. My mother also shared her good fortune with the community by supporting five older women from the area who lived at the Buddhist monastery. She gave money and food to them on the first of every month.

My mother educated us in her ways. She told us to help others out when they are in need, to always be polite and to be kind because one day the people you help out will return the favor. My mother said that the family is like the fingers on your hand. All these fingers come off of one hand; some tall, some short, some smart, some rich, and some poor in life - we all come from the same hand - we are all here to help each other. Someone in heaven sent us here to become a family, to become brothers, sisters, a mother, a father and just like a hand we have to stay together and help each other stay family.

In 1973 my father bought a house, which was an extraordinary achievement and a great thing for our family. It was 31 meters deep (99 feet) and four and a half stories high. I carry a vivid memory of loading the money for the house onto my bicycle trailer and riding home to count the money. I had never seen so much money. My father had saved all his life for this house. He wanted his family to be secure. Now that he had a house and a thriving restaurant business to pass on to his children, he knew he and my mother would one day be able to retire comfortably. At least that was the plan. At that time, our future life seemed secure with endless possibilities.

GROWING UP

Cambodia seemed to be a veritable paradise when I was young. The sun was out every day unless it was monsoon season. Without fail the temperature was usually about 80 degrees Fahrenheit and very humid. We were outside as much as we could be; even when it rained we were outside. The clouds would appear, maybe the wind would blow, and then rain poured from the sky. Sometimes it rained so hard you could see the drops bouncing back off of the street. We would play a game with the rain and run out from where we hid to avoid the downpour. Once out in the rain we would look up and open our eyes to stare straight up to the sky. At times the rain was falling so hard it hurt to hit your face and the game would be "how long can you stand the pain". It would rain hard for fifteen or twenty minutes and magically the sun would reappear from behind the clouds and dry everything out.

We had our family and we were close as close could be. I was able to run around our house and the neighborhood. Because my parents knew everyone around us we could travel the streets and people would look after us. I can remember this as being magical. I remember we were always wearing shorts just like my father did. I never saw him out of a pair of shorts.

I was pretty active when I was young so my parents sent me to school when I was five. But I wasn't a big fan of school at the time and kept running away. I would wait until no one was looking at me and then sneak out an open window or door and run for home. Once I was out of the school grounds I would slow down and look at all the street vendors hawking their wares along the way. I was rebellious and easily bored and couldn't sit still for long without my mind wandering.

When I was six years old, I joined the lion dance troupe (also known as the dragon dance), which performed after Chinese New Year to raise money for schools. And that's when I discovered how much I loved to be in front of people and perform. I was happiest in front of a crowd, acting crazy and trying to make them laugh. For a long time after that, I thought I wanted to be a comedian. I was also a part of the annual Chinese Opera and I took great pride in being a member of the Chinese funeral band.

Lion Dance Group. I am the little one in the front row.

Being from a family that ran their own business the entrepreneurial spirit was in me from a very young age. When I was eight years old I started my first business, selling water to passengers on a neighbor's bus that traveled out to the small towns. I saved money just like my parents had trained me to do and I even gave some of the money away to the old people in the community. I also walked around town and collected and sold empty bottles. When I wanted to reward myself I would buy my favorite treat: grilled bananas. I can still recall their smoky flavor and the decadent little sprinkling of sugar on them. During summer vacations I used to stand out in front of the movie theater selling candies. I also worked the public market selling cookies and breads. Also, I used the money to buy clothes and shoes for my upcoming school year.

Although I was a good kid and knew how to earn money, I was also very mischevious. I have one very vivid memory of getting into trouble at my Aunt's house when I was 11 years old. She used to take in boarders to earn a little extra money. She had one fellow who rented a room downstairs and I watched him for several days after he moved in and I noticed when he came home he hung his work pants on the wall on a hook. From time to time I would walk casually through his room, say "Hi" to him and check out the money that was hanging out of his pocket. I worked up the nerve to start stealing the money from his pocket so I would sneak into his room when no one was around, stick my hand in there, take the money and run like hell out of my Aunt's house. Even though I was stealing money from him I never took all it, I would just take a little of it to buy some stuff like candy or whatever.

After a couple of weeks, he realized that someone had been stealing from his pocket so he set up an ambush.

One day, I saw his pants hanging on the hook near his mosquito net and I went to take the money and he jumped out of the net with his brother. They both caught me in the act of stealing. I was done for and I knew I was in trouble. Real trouble because they knew my father and this was going to really upset him. They went and talked with my father and when I got home later that night my father tore into me. He beat the living hell out of me and then chained me up around the neck to a table in the house. My father said "So you want to be a criminal do you? This is what will happen to you in prison; they will lock you up around the neck and beat you all the time". After this punishment I realized that I did not have any desire to ever be a criminal. My father asked me how much I stole from him. I was not sure how much I actually took so I just mentioned a number and he gave me the money to give back to the fellow and told me to apologize to him. I went to my aunt's house and did what my father told me to do. I told him I was really sorry and that I would not be stealing ever again.

Although the restaurant was a success, times were still tough for my family and everyone worked all the time. If we were old enough to work we either helped our parents in the restaurant or looked after our younger siblings. Even though life was extremely busy I have fond memories of those days. I graduated from school at the age of 14 and immediately started to learn how to cook at our restaurant. After closely observing the cooks for a while, I was allowed to help them chop vegetables and cut meat. I learned how to slaughter chickens. I had to be really fast or the older cooks would get mad and throw things at me. I learned quickly because I didn't want to get burned by whatever they threw. Soon the cooks saw my enthusiasim and started to teach me more advanced techniques and how to prepare specific dishes. When I was 15, I became a salaried employee, working all positions. Everyone in the family had something to do in that place, and we were all proud to be part of it.

One day, when I was 16, the cook didn't show up for work at the restaurant. I knew this was my big chance, so I just walked into the kitchen and started cooking. My dad told me if I didn't know how to do something, to just walk away from it. I told him to just watch me. I cooked my heart out and kept up with all the orders that were flying into the kitchen that day. Later, he told my mom, "Hey, he ain't too bad!" After this foray into the front lines, I became the official back-up cook. Whenever someone was sick or on vacation, I took that person's place in the kitchen.

Another favorite memory of those years was the movies. I loved all kinds, but cowboy-and-Indian movies were a big favorite. After work, my friends and I would get together and learn the latest pop songs from the U.S. and smoke cigarettes, trying to be cool like the people we saw in the movies. Sometimes our little pack would ride our motorcycles over to eat French food. We'd hop back on our vehicles, start the engines up, rev them loudly and ride off, hair flying in the wind, shirts open, thinking we were as cool as James Dean. I had a good-sized motorcycle, a Kawasaki 100 cc, and it was my freedom machine. I used to fly on that motorcycle! I acted the tough guy on a bike just like in the movies.

Clint Eastwood was my favorite movie actor during those years. When a new Clint Eastwood film arrived in town, I had to be the first to see it. I loved the way Clint held that cigar in his mouth, how his eye would twitch when he got mad at someone, how he would say a line just right. Even though he said little, the words spoke volumes to me and made his characters larger than life itself.

Sometimes I just sat in the theater all day long, watching the same movie over and over again. I'd learn all the lines and repeat them back while the characters spoke. People in my family would call me a movie freak and I would respond by giving them the Clint snarl. You know the one, where he kind of curls up one side of his lip and gives you that cold, cold stare. I would stand in front of a mirror and practice the snarl until I thought I was doing it as well as Clint. When I started smoking, I made sure that I stood the same way as Clint and lit my cigarette in the same off-hand way. I had it all down.

I liked plenty of other American things as well. I also loved tie-dyed T-shirts and the Beach Boys. I really liked rock and roll that had a good beat. Without even knowing exactly what surfing was, we thought it was about the coolest thing ever. When a surfing movie finally came out, we were blown away by the young people on the screen riding the waves. To my friends and me in Cambodia this was amazing. And after this brief escape from reality, it was always back to work at the restaurant and life in Cambodia.

My late teens were among the happiest times in my life. I knew how to hustle to make money, and I had a little freedom.

My friends and I were always racing bikes together, pushing each other to go faster and pull crazier moves.

I was an energetic and hotheaded teenager and still learning how to control my own temper, which tended to flare up at inopportune moments. I once had a run-in with a police officer that really made me clean up my act. I realized my actions could bring shame upon my family and I knew I didn't want that. This police officer came to the restaurant and asked me to run across the street to buy him some cigarettes. When I brought them back, he claimed they weren't fresh and sent me back for a different pack. He did this several times and started cursing and yelling. I lost my head and grabbed a soy sauce bottle to throw at him. My mother stopped me in the nick of time. After this episode, I tried much harder to rein in my emotions and consider the consequences of my actions—not always easy, but I did my best.

The most tragic and defining event for our family during my teenage years was the death of my little sister Muy, who caught a high fever that struck down many young people across Cambodia. Overwhelmed with sadness, my father stopped working and started drinking, which brought on liver trouble and high blood pressure.

Aside from the loss of my sister and the concern about my father's declining health, I was a pretty carefree and happy teen who didn't give much thought to the future. I had some money from my work, my motorcycle, my pack of friends, my suave Clint Eastwood moves, and life was good.

THE ARRIVAL OF
THE KHMER ROUGE

The Khmer Rouge first appeared on the Cambodian national scene in 1970 and was started by a man named Pol Pot who actually got their name from the deposed Prince Sihanouk. In the mid 1970's Prince Sihanouk left the country for surgery and the leader of the country's army staged a coup against the Prince. General Lon Nol turned out to be a very cruel leader and inept leader. With his army mired in corruption and incompetence the Khmer Rouge began to win battles against the Cambodian army. As the war raged on for 5 years the tenacity in which the Khmer Rouge army fought amazed even seasoned veterans. In many small villages and towns in the countryside the legend of the tough Khmer Rouge soldier grew quickly and with that legend the Khmer Rouge gained more support both in the country side and in the larger cities.

By early 1975, having lost support amongst most of the civilian population and with the Khmer Rouge literally chasing him from the country by shooting rockets at his plane General Lon Nol fled the country. From within the besieged capital, Phnom Penh, Premier Long Boret offered to surrender on the sole condition that there be no reprisals against those who had stayed loyal to the Cambodian government. The Khmer Rouge refused and the government had no choice but to surrender.

We awoke one morning in early spring of 1975 to the sound of machine gun fire and realized the war for the soul of Cambodia had come to our sleepy city. As the front lines of the battle got closer to Battambang, everyone in the city began to realize that the Khmer Rouge were shooting rockets towards us. The closer the front line got the explosions sounded bigger and became more ominous. Frightened, we turned on the radio to see what was going on outside of our city. There was nothing playing on the radio except classical music that day which struck me as odd because usually someone was announcing the news. Several hours later a voice came on and told us that the capital city of Phnom Penh had fallen to the Khmer Rouge invaders.

I knew Battambang would be next and indeed it was. On April 15th 1975, the Khmer Rouge circled Battambang and launched several missiles into the middle of the city, instantly destroying several buildings. At that point, the Khmer Rouge sent an emissary to persuade the governor to surrender the city to their army. He was told if he did not give up, the Khmer Rouge would launch one thousand missiles and level the entire city. I will remember the day for the rest of my life. When the missiles exploded in the center of town many of us ran to see what damage they had done. My brothers and I got to the street in a hurry and ran towards the billowing smoke.

We saw people walking out of buildings with their skin hanging off of them and saw others lying on the street wailing out in pain from the loss of a leg or an arm.

One man was staggering down the street holding onto his stomach, which was bleeding profusely. I turned and looked at him only to realize he was trying in vain to hold his intestine and stomach in his body with one hand. Others looked like they had been blown out of the buildings that had been hit by the rockets. What was left of their bodies strewn about like so much junk. Blood was everywhere and the smell of burning flesh hung in the air. Word soon spread to others around Battambang about the destruction of the buildings and the loss of life. This created a pall that fell over the city as a whole and you could sense the fear in the air. As I sat there on the sidewalk looking at the whole scene I was struck hard as if someone had hit me in the head with a hammer. My brothers found me and told me we had to get home as quick as possible.

Once we got home our family stayed in the house, locked the doors, and from the relative safety of the third floor, we watched from the windows as people kicked in the doors of businesses on our street and ran off with their arms full of whatever they could carry. Some of them fought with each other, hitting each other in the head or back with scraps of metal or bricks to beat the others into the shops. Our minds swirled with confusion as the night was pierced with blood-curdling screams. We did not know what to make of all of this. What did it mean to our family? What did it mean for our country? Where was all of this headed? We sat in shocked silence as we watched our beloved town fall into total chaos.

The crowd soon arrived at the public market right across from the restaurant, and started looting and tearing up the market. The first wave of looters grabbed clothes, food and liquor, whatever they could lay their hands on, and ran. The next wave, seeing there wasn't much left, started to break the stalls down by kicking at the beams that supported them. It was pandemonium, and yet we could do nothing. We were so struck with horror by the savagery and violence of it all.

No one tried to stop the madness, as the Khmer Rouge soldiers themselves were among the looters. In one instance, some Khmer Rouge soldiers opened up the grains warehouse and actually invited people to take as much rice as they could carry. Meanwhile, other soldiers were trying to restore a semblance of order and were shooting looters on sight. Still others danced around, happy that the war was finally over, as they believed this would usher in a new era of peace.

Amid all the chaos, we hardly knew what to think. We got practical and began by gathering supplies from our restaurant. We dashed to and from as quickly as we could and we made sure to travel in pairs. One person carried what they could on their backs and the other was to ward off any robbers. All of the brothers took turns running back and forth from the restaurant to the house. My father directed us to grab as much rice and canned goods as could in case we were confined to the house.

After several hours of running back and forth from the restaurant I took some time to talk with my brother. I said to him "Let's go to the association and get the drums and do the lion dance to celebrate peace!" But my brother didn't think that would be a good idea. My father startled us all when he stated that he thought this was going to be a bad thing for the country and for our family as well. Surveying the chaos on all sides, he said (with great accuracy, it turns out); "This is the end of an era. Our time is over and things will never be the same." My older brothers were all silent, in shock at what had happened to our little town in just a few short hours and dismayed at how quickly the veil of civility had been ruptured. Their silence was ominous—and contagious. We sat together and waited to see what would happen next.

On April 18th the Khmer Rouge soldiers started to rob the jewelry stores. For some reason we could never figure out, the Khmer Rouge were obsessed with expensive watches. The looting continued, but now people focused especially on grocery stores. People were suddenly very afraid and not knowing what was going to happen next, they started hoarding whatever they could get their hands on.

The next day the Khmer Rouge soldiers came around and started telling people that they had to leave the city right away because the Americans were going to bomb it. They shot their guns in the air and literally chased the locals out of our hometown. I heard through the grapevine that the soldiers rounded up all of the government soldiers in trucks, drove them out to the outskirts of town, and killed them all on the spot. The generals and their underlings were told that Prince Sihanouk had come home and that they should all go to the airport to welcome him back. The Khmer Rouge loaded them up and, again, killed them all. A friend of ours who had joined the Khmer Rouge told me, "No one trusts anyone. I cannot even trust my own bodyguard. If I do anything the leadership does not like, I will be killed too. You must prepare your family for whatever happens. And whatever they say, do not trust anyone!"

We knew we could depend on what he told us as being the truth because he had worked at our restaurant and had become a trusted family friend. It was our understanding that he decided to join the Khmer Rouge only after the Cambodian army had bombed his home village that killed his wife and only son.

When the Khmer Rouge told everyone we were only leaving town for three days, I knew that was a lie. I told my family, "Let's pack up all the valuable stuff and all the food we can carry as well." I went to a bicycle rental store and managed to get my hands on 2 bicycle carts. We filled them with everything we thought we might need—sacks of rice, oil, flour and clothes, and all the gold my father had hidden in the house. My family and I rode away from our house out to a Muslim village about 3 kilometers west out of Battambang, where my mother knew some people she had helped out in the past. While the women and children settled in the village, the men in the family did multiple trips back into town, ferrying things out to the village.

Each trip took about an hour because there were so many people leaving in a hurry, all heading away as fast as their feet could carry them. As I made my last trip out of the city before the 5:00 p.m. deadline, I took a moment to look back at our house and started to cry. I was so confused it felt as if my head was spinning. My father had worked so hard for this house and now we won't be able to live in it. Our restaurant, my father's pride and joy, gone with the winds of change. It was then it all came crashing down on me. I sat down in the street and let the tears fall. The more I cried the more I felt free from the stress of it all. I knew my family was waiting for me so I left and joined them and headed up river where my mother's friends lived.

Situated alongside the Stunt Sangker River that runs through and around Battambang, the Muslim village we were in was home to about two thousand people and there were many people we knew from our neighborhood as well as our restaurant. Even though life was far from normal, the familiar faces allowed us to enjoy some small sense of community there. Of course, familiar faces or not, life ultimately came to be dominated by our fear of the Khmer Rouge, and we had to be very careful about talking too much. I remember hearing about one fellow who was talking about the old days in Battambang and how he enjoyed going to have noodles and coffee with friends every morning.

Word got back to the soldiers that he was talking about the old days. The soldiers tracked him down and killed him on the spot. Since no one knew precisely what could get you killed, we became fearful and mistrustful of everyone at all times, even those we'd known for a long time. We all knew people who had suddenly disappeared from our lives. One day they were there working alongside you in the fields, and the next day, they were gone. We quickly learned that the only solution was to keep quiet, trust no one, and try to remain invisible.

Although we showed up at their doorstep without any warning, my mother's friend graciously took us in without hesitation, only asking that we respect their religion and not slaughter any pigs on their property. Despite some difficult moments when we first arrived—due primarily to the fact that neither family knew much about the other's religious practices— we were grateful for a place to stay as we figured out what was going on. Thanks to them, our family actually managed to settle into a tenuous sense of normalcy despite the chaos swirling around the countryside at that time.

While we stayed with the Muslim family we felt the right thing to do was to help out by working in their rice fields which were situated about three kilometers outside of town. We left early every morning and worked until 5:00 p.m. We planted rice all day long in anticipation of the rainy season. We had to dig the soil with hoes, as there was no machinery or cows. We dug and dug all day long. I'd never done this kind of back-breaking manual labor before, having spent most of my working life in the restaurant, it was hard work.

Many nights, random Khmer Rouge soldiers would show up out of nowhere and ask us to hand over the food supplies that we had brought with us. They especially wanted the rum. We'd already seen and heard enough to know they'd kill us on the spot if we refused. We did as we were told, trying not to panic about our rapidly diminishing stockpile. Our family had to be careful to not alienate these fellows. The Khmer Rouge wanted to eliminate anyone suspected of "involvement in free market activities". Suspected capitalists encompassed professionals and almost everyone with an education, many urban dwellers, and people with connections to foreign governments. All they had to do was accuse one of us of being a spy or of having money and that would be sufficient justification to get rid of us. The younger soldiers completely bought in to the Khmer Rouge's propaganda. Not only did we have to worry about being city dwellers but the Khmer Rouge had particular contempt for those of Chinese descent (like us), claiming that we were not really Cambodian at heart and therefore disposable.

I woke up one morning and felt very sick to my stomach. I could hardly get up, yet I still had to drag myself out to the fields and toil away all day long. Our Muslim friends were afraid that I was going to die in the rice fields and tried to talk the soldiers into allowing me to have some time off to heal but the Khmer Rouge wanted everyone planting rice every day and saying no to them was simply not an option. If you were brazen enough to stand up to them for any reason, they'd just pull you out of line and kill you right there in front of everyone to drive home the point that they were to be obeyed at all times.

Even though I was passing blood 30 or 40 times a day, I continued to plant rice. Whatever it was (most likely food poisoning of some kind), it almost killed me. I lost about 3 inches of body fat around my waist within a few days. This sickness dragged on for two full weeks greatly depleting my body and spirit. I couldn't understand how my life had changed so suddenly. I was spending my days bent over in the fields, drinking filthy and contaminated water, wearing the Khmer Rouge-issued black clothing, with the sun beating down on my back all day; and surviving on only the paltriest nourishment. Back in Battambang, only a few weeks ago my friends called me "Fat boy," but now I was skinny as a rail.

My mother was finally able to trade some food for medicine because there was a thriving black market among people who had managed to hang on to their stash of supplies. The Khmer Rouge was still getting organized and had not yet locked us down to the point where they controlled every aspect of our daily lives. After taking the medicine, I recovered within a couple of days.

My father, being the generous man he was, gave away our supplies to old friends who would come by and ask. The friends wanted to give him gold in exchange, but my father refused the gold and just gave them what they asked for out of the kindness of his heart. His saying was "every time you helped someone out, you were planting a good seed in their lives that would repay you later." We were concerned with our dwindling supplies, but there was little we could do to stop him.

We gathered the family and talked with our father about moving once again. We all felt we should waste no time. There were rumors floating around about how the Khmer Rouge was starting to monitor every move people made. So we packed up our belongings and moved up towards Wat Ek Phnom where we knew a family. The move was nine kilometers away so we traded some of our liquor and food for the use of an ox and a cart. Once we got to our friend's the only place for us was under the house which was built on poles about 10 feet off of the ground in case of flooding during the monsoon rains. Unfortunately, our situation didn't change as much as we'd hoped it would. Here too, the Khmer Rouge soldiers would come by at night and ask us for things. Again, they wanted rum the most (even though they were supposedly against drinking alcohol). It was just more of the same in a new place.

As the Khmer Rouge started to institute more and more control over our every move they began to build small stations which were positioned just outside the villages. They lived in the stations and patrolled the villages at night, selecting people to kill or taking whatever they wanted. Since you never knew when they might appear at your house, this made life very tense.

To make matters worse, we were constantly hearing rumors of Khmer Rouge brutality. We heard stories around the old village that the Khmer Rouge would just pick a family at random and destroy the family one by one, taking one parent one night, another the next, and so on. The remaining members of the family would huddle together at night, clinging to each other, not knowing who would be taken away next.

The temple at Wat Ek Phonm

The insanity would continue into the next day when you had to go to work in the rice fields, fighting your hunger the entire day. The soldiers kept everyone on edge with their cruel unpredictability. You might come home to discover that your family had been beaten that day, or you might witness a fellow worker being shot or hacked to death for not having bowed low enough or for having made eye contact with a soldier. It was safest to walk with our heads down, shoulders hunched over, so as to avoid any human contact. This at least enabled us to insulate ourselves from the insanity swirling all around us and to protect the family for at least a couple more hours. We learned quickly. For instance, you wanted to avoid contact with the soldiers who carried guns at all costs as they were known to shoot on sight. Sometimes, the soldiers would try to trick people by chatting them up, asking their name or what group we were from. If they made the mistake of replying, they were killed. Apparently, the Khmer Rouge was cleaning the "undesirables" out of society as efficiently as they could. They were so ruthless and cruel to so many that it was getting increasingly difficult to understand who would be left after they were done.

THE EARLY MONTHS: WORK, WORK AND MORE WORK

As the Khmer Rouge got more organized, our lives became ever more regimented and scheduled. People were assigned to different groups, which were responsible for performing certain tasks. Some dug ditches, some made dams, and others (depending on the season) planted rice. My older brothers, for instance, were assigned to go to the forest to cut wood and bamboo. Those who were married were assigned work closer to the village. If you were single, they sent you out to the remotest areas.

Regardless of where you were, or what you were doing, the work was without exception back-breaking and continuous. We worked daily from 6:00 a.m. to 11:00 a.m. and from 1:00 p.m. to 5:00 p.m. There was never any breakfast so we ate for the first time each day after 11:00 a.m. At the end of the day, we were given another small meal. During rainy season, this consisted of rice soup (rice boiled in water), and during the dry season (also called planting season), we subsisted on hard cooked rice. It hardly mattered because it was so hot during planting season you could not really eat anything anyway. The meals were all communal, and the food we received was equal to how many people were in the group. If there were 10 people then each person received one can of rice and the can used to measure the rice was a 14 ounce condensed milk can. In our village, we had one ladle of rice soup for lunch and one ladle for dinner. Every so often we would receive one little chunk of meat usually about the size of a persons thumb and since we had not eaten any meat in so long people would get sick from the fat in the meat.

Although it often involved walking an extra mile or two each way, it was better to be assigned work as far as possible from the village because you got double rations. Also, when you were away from the camp, you had a little more freedom to walk around. Inside the village itself, every moment had become measured and you were monitored all the time. We could not go for a walk without explaining to the group leader where we were going. My guess was they wanted to keep us busy so that we might actually forget we were starving all the time. We never really learned the greater purpose of our work—or even what the Khmer Rouge wanted for the country itself. We were only told what our specific task was—and we knew better than to ask questions.

I was resting one day after working in the rice fields and was told that I was being assigned to dig a road across the rice fields. I no longer remember how long the road was, but it seemed endless. There were thousands of us out there digging all day long. It was the dry time of year, and the sun beat down on us mercilessly. We had no clean water to drink. We dug until our hands split open, and we had to pry our fingers off the shovel. And when we stood up, it took some time to straighten out our shoulders, which had locked into a hunched stoop as we dug.

Every once in a while, when the guards where not looking, we would take a chance and stand up and stretch our backs out to ease the pain a bit. At the end of the day, we were so exhausted that our only thought was of lying down and sleeping. Many around us were so exhausted they openly burst into tears from exhaustion.

Village life came to be centered on meetings with the other groups in the area. Each group consisted of fifty to one hundred families, and each village was home to eight or nine groups. Once a week, there were group meetings, and once a month on Sundays, there was a village meeting. At the meetings, the soldiers mostly informed us that we needed to work harder to get more rice cultivated. They would pick out people in our group and claim they had done something against Angka, the ruling party of Cambodia. Of course, there were never any written rules about what would or would not offend Angka, so we never knew if what we were doing or saying was against Angka or not. At the end of these meetings, the Khmer Rouge would drag these people away, and I can only assume that most were tortured or killed.

At our first meeting, they brought a pregnant woman up to the front because she had stolen food from her neighbor. The Khmer Rouge explained stealing was against the law and their solution was to get rid of people like that. One of the soldiers walked her out of the crowd to the temple's fence. A few minutes later, he returned with her towel and her shirt around his shoulder, which meant he had killed her. Although nothing was said explicitly, everyone knew what had happened. I could hardly bear to look at this man. You could tell by the evil glint in his eye he took pleasure in killing and he savored the satisfaction of being good at what he did. The only way to protect ourselves was to continue to work hard, stay quiet, and do our best to remain anonymous.

They were brilliant at creating an atmosphere of mistrust. One of their tactics was to tell us if one member of the group did something against Angka and nobody else reported the wrong doing, they would kill the entire group. This basically meant you couldn't talk to anyone. So there was little comfort or support to be had from anyone else in your group. Your only option was to keep to yourself and your family.

Some families even had to monitor the actions of the children. The Khmer Rouge were expert at indoctrinating the children, as the little ones were the most open to their radical ideas. Children would run and tell the Khmer Rouge of the "bad actions" of the parent and that parent would disappear, never to be seen again.

Fear and doubt permeated every conversation. It made all of us crazy because you did not know who you could talk to. I think it's important to explain here that going to a coffee house, sitting down and enjoying coffee and bread, and talking about the day with people you do not know was an important part of Cambodian culture. To not be able to talk openly and engage in conversation was a devastating blow to our way of life. Terrified of initiating even the shortest conversation, we simply severed all ties to each other, going so far as to avoid even making eye contact. It is hard to describe how exhausting, demoralizing, and crushing it is to live every day in fear of your fellow man.

Another clever Khmer Rouge tactic was to separate families: the elderly, the married, the young, and the teens all went to different places. In Cambodia, the family is the core unit of everyone's life, and the cruelest thing they could do was break down the family unit. By destroying family ties, they further weakened our ability to fight back. My family was spared some of the pain that others had to endure. My sister, for instance, was married and was able to stay in the village near my parents. My mother and father were able to stay together because my father was sick and they put my mother in charge of cooking and looking after the youngest of the children in the village who were not strong enough to do manual labor.

My older brothers were sent out to work in the forest for long periods of time and were able to come home from time to time. I was sent out to plant rice and chop down bamboo and was able to come back home at the end of my scheduled work day. My younger brothers were lucky in that they were not reassigned somewhere else. I do not know why things worked out like they did for my family, but it was one of the very few blessings during that time. I always thought my grandparents were watching us from above and taking care of us and I always prayed to my grandparents to watch over the family.

One day, a couple of my friends came to me in the fields and said, "Hey there are only a couple of soldiers with guns. We can overcome them, kill them, take the guns and run west to Thailand." But I told them, "That is no good because our families would pay the price for us killing the soldiers. It is better to be cool." People in the village were always talking with those they thought they could trust about ways to escape or to fight back, but really there was no way. Any sort of uprising would have been brutally punished. I was always telling people it is better to do as they say, keep your head down and wait to live to see another day. The sun would rise again on Cambodia if we could stay alive. This became my motto as I dug and dug through each day. In my heart, I knew that this kind of life could not go on forever.

After a month or so in Wat Ek Phnom, my family decided to move again. We were getting nervous about our diminishing supplies—which were crucial to helping us survive—and felt we'd be better off in a village where no one knew that we had anything. So we packed up our belongings and made the trip to Wat Bote Wung, which is closer to Battambang.

Since Wat Bote Wung was about 3 kilometers north of Battambang, I took a chance and snuck back in to the city to visit our house and to see what had become of our old neighborhood. I was stunned to discover that the city had been entirely abandoned. And I'm not exaggerating. There was not a single person left. It was a ghost town, so quiet that I could hear the echoes of my flip flops resounding as I walked the city blocks. I was very afraid that I was going to run into a soldier or two patrolling the city, but I saw no signs of any military presence. It was very eerie, and I had to be careful not to get caught, as the Khmer Rouge would have slit my throat on the spot if they'd found me prowling around.

In the house of a former neighbor, I found a large box of matches and in another house a few silver coins but I could not find any food. Anything that had been left behind had already been taken. I took the matches, figuring that I'd be able to trade them for something else later on and I knew I could trade the silver coins for rice. When I made it to our old house, the place had been cleaned out: all of our furniture, knick knacks and everything of any value at all. I was suddenly incredibly sad. It tore a big whole in my heart because I knew for certain I was never going to be able to return to my old life. The past was irretrievable, and I was going to have to accept this horrific new life as my reality.

The Khmer Rouge viewed us as garbage. We often heard them saying "killing one of you is like taking out the garbage." Our lives simply had no value to them. I often thought they said things like that to continue the collective societal breakdown, which was aimed at both the psychological and physical self. I can think of no other reason. We were already essentially posessionless. We heard the speeches from the leaders telling us that owning anything is bad, if we have the desire to own we are thinking not in the Angkar mind but with the capitalistic mind and if we are thinking in those terms we need to have our thinking "corrected". The word corrected here can be substituted for torture. This meant being tied up and beaten until you confess to them you are a spy for either the CIA or the Vietnamese or whatever insanity the Khmer Rouge was trying to rid their "perfect" society of. Their need to torture and kill us seemed to change with the weather. It was as if the leadership was inventing situations so they could have a reason to kill even more of us. As if they needed a reason for that.

By far my least favorite job during our stay in Wat Bote Wung was cleaning the waste out of the sewer ditch. I had to jump waist deep and scoop it out with a basket. I really cannot describe the smell of human waste in 100 degree heat that has been sitting and stewing away for months. I can only say that every time I got near to the ditch I wanted to vomit. The smell hung in the air so thickly it seemed to permeate every thing around it. Once you jumped in that ditch flies descended on you like some unholy plague from hell and would not leave you alone because once you got out you smelled like what you were just in. No matter how hard I tried to get the smell off of me and out of my nose I could not. I tried wearing a *gama* over my face and that did not work. I tried stuffing my nose with whatever I could find and still I could smell that noxious stew. I performed this demeaning task for about a week and developed a serious rash on the lower part of my body. There were obviously no medications, but a villager told me to mix a certain kind of leaf with salt and apply it to the rash. Both the rash and the leaf mixture were incredibly painful.

One day in the community headquarters, near the warehouse I found some used motor oil and decided to try and use that on the rash. I looked around to make sure that no one was watching me and I scooped out small can full of the oil and went and put it on my rash. At first the rash escalated into a very bad infection, but after two days, I felt better so I went back to the oil can, scooped out some more oil and reapplied it on the rash. I kept on applying the oil for about a month until the rash eventually disappeared. There were added benefits to the motor oil as well. When I applied the motor oil to my legs it helped keep the leeches off of my legs when I had to work in the sewage ditch.

After we cleaned the ditch our next assigned job was to dig in the rice fields. The rice field was around 5 or 6 acres square. The water was pumped out of the field and we had to dig the mud out of the field to enlarge the area and dig it deeper. Again this was all done by hand using hoes and buckets. There were hundreds of us doing this task. I think it took us about 1 week to get this done.

There were about 5 or 6 of us in one area of the rice fields digging away and we hit something very hard down in the mud. We bent over and to our surprise, pulled up a clay jar and bones. I think it may have been an ancient burial ground of some sort. Suddenly we saw a bunch of red stones about the size of my thumb and in the middle of the stone was a 6 angle cut where you could put a chain or a string through. I grabbed those stones and kept them, and I also found a stone bracelet about the size of someone's wrist. I wore them around my neck with a piece of nylon string attached to it.

While we were working in the rice field we had to sleep near our assigned work areas. There were times when there weren't many trees to fashion a hammock so we were forced to sleep in the mud. We would try and push the grass down as much as we could to make the base for a bed and put our grass rug over the top of the grass. We had to be careful not to roll because there was mud all around us and of course mud and swamp means mosquitoes. Our feet would be so covered in mud at the end of the day and we were so tired and sore from bending over all day it was easiest to just go to sleep with muddy feet. There was no reason to knock the mud off because the next day we were going to be out in the fields doing the same damned thing.

After working in the rice field I was assigned to a job about 24 kilometers away from the village, chopping tall grass. The area was teeming with snakes, and I really hated snakes. One night, the backpack that a fellow worker was using as a pillow started to move around under his head. He screamed when he spotted a cobra beneath his head. Fortunately for us, one fellow knew how to grab cobras so he just grabbed the cobra and killed it. The next day we all shared in eating the cobra. Even though it was snake it was meat and it had been a while since we had some protein.

After resting a good while we took off and went about 5 kilometers and I came across a fellow that I knew from Battambang and he said that they moved many families to the Wat Ga Go village and my family was amongst those that got reassigned. I walked from where we were to Wat Ga Go village and found my family alongside the road sitting near a grain storage shed. This was to be our house while we lived in Wat Ga Go. The whole family which included 15 people, nieces, nephews, brothers and my parents stayed in a small area about 20 ft by 20 ft. We had no beds to sleep on so we just slept on little grass rugs and curled up next to each other. We were fortunate because we still had a small stash of supplies from when we left Battambang. Of course, once again the Khmer Rouge chlubs (spies) knew we still had supplies and they would stop by and demand that we give them whatever they asked for.

During our stay in Wat Ga Go I was able to use my language skills to speak both Cambodian and Chinese. I was called upon to look after the other Chinese in the village who did not speak the language. They saw me as the defacto point man to deal with the Cambodian-speaking villagers. Whenever there was trouble between the Cambodians and Chinese cultures, I became the mediator. Eventually, the Cambodians in the area came to respect me because of my knowledge of their culture. Sometimes certain Cambodians would try and pick fights with the Chinese by calling us *Jun*, which is a very derogatory term. This made the hot heads in the Chinese group want to fight. I would settle everyone down by telling them that we need to all get along now and when the Khmer Rouge ask you to do something do it. I told them that we all need to stay alive and we all need to work and stay together.

In our village we had to go to the main grains storage warehouse every evening to get our rice for the next day. When the rice was weighed out by the soldiers, I made sure the soldiers could not see me as I very slowly moved my finger underneath the scale so the rice would not seem to weigh as much. That way, everyone got more than the allotted portion of rice. I did this for everyone in the camp, essentially risking my life to make sure people in the camp got more food, so everyone really liked me. In this way, I felt like a little bit less of a victim. I still managed to control my destiny in small ways.

Grains Warehouse where our family lived
(still standing as of April 2010)

As time wore on, averting all-out starvation became the only thing on our minds. By this time our reserves had been utterly depleted and it was nearly impossible to subsist on a couple of cans of rice a day. We did not think of the future, or the past, only the now of starving. And despite our weakness, we still had to get up and work every day because the Khmer Rouge believed if you did not work you should get less food than the ones who were working. The only choice we had was to keep going. When I was in charge of handing out the rice for the groups I made sure everyone got their full share, even if they weren't feeling well. I felt bad for everyone in the village but there was little else I could do.

While in Wat Ga Go my 15-year-old brother Chai was sent off to join a teenager's group. The Khmer Rouge knew they could exert the most influence on the youngest members of society and once they'd been converted to their cause, they could use them to break down loyalty and trust within families. By brainwashing the young they could effectively destroy the tight knit fabric of the Cambodian family.

Chai did not like this programming, so he escaped from the young persons group and returned home. When he arrived at our little hut, his watchers were not far behind. They arrived, beat Chai in front of my mother and father, and took him back. My father was heartbroken, sick over the fact that he could do nothing to help his son. After Chai was taken away, my father changed. I understood how he felt. I, too, was utterly powerless. In the old days when someone crossed a family member like that, I had always defended my family in whatever way seemed appropriate. Loyalty was everything to me.

What could I do in this situation? Who could I find to take my frustration out on? I had to hide the anger deep inside me and pretend it didn't matter to me. In my head, I pledged to myself that if and when the Khmer Rouge was ever overthrown, I was going to find someone to take out my hatred on. Of course not everything I was thinking was of hatred and killing.

I was confronted from time to time with beauty when I saw the desire of my heart and seeing her became one of my few pleasant memories. I remember one day in particular because she ended up working with me digging ditches. I was in the ditch with a hoe and she was taking the dirt that I dug, putting it in a basket and hauling it up the side of the ditch. I would look up at her and steal a glance from time to time.

When our digging duties were done, we climbed up a tree and started talking, pretending that we were picking berries. I made sure no one was looking and I asked her her name. She told me her name was Hong, which in Chinese means Phoenix, like the bird rising. You see, we had to talk like we were working on something because the Khmer Rouge did not like boys and girls talking with each other. We could have gotten into big trouble, maybe even killed from just this simple interaction. Every time I said something to her, she smiled a beautiful smile that melted my heart. I felt all warm inside, and the only thing I could do was smile back at her to show her my affection through eye contact. It was there in that tree that I decided I would ask her to marry me.

Since we were both in the same village, we kept on seeing each other around the worksites and camp. I finally worked up the nerve to ask her to marry me. She politely told me that I had to go ask her parents. Since I did not know her parents, I asked my father to go talk with her father, whom my father knew from Battambang. But her father told him, "No he can't, because the village chief's son is already asking about marrying her." I was saddened by this, but we ended up staying friends. We couldn't risk doing anything to displease the village chief.

THE ONGOING
HUNT FOR FOOD

I n the early spring of 1976 when the rainy season began, we moved to the Ou Ta Ki area to work in the fields there. During this time the group I was with had even less than the usual small allotment of food. 1976 was especially bad for starvation under the Khmer Rouge. People were literally dying all the time. When we went to sleep at night (if we could sleep at all because of empty bellies) we were never sure who would wake up in the morning. We had to find whatever we could to eat. People were eating anything they could find to fill their stomachs. Grass, leaves, tree bark, no matter what, if it was edible we ate it.

One very desperate night I snuck out and walked to Phnom Sampov, a hilly area about 15 kilometers away. We would have been killed outright if we'd been caught sneaking out, but, we had to get our hands on some food. I brought along some of my stash of matches, and we cut across the flooded rice fields between Ou Ta Ki and Phnom Sampov. When we got to the village, I traded the matches for rice (their rations were a relatively luxurious three cans of rice per day, so they were willing to give some up). We spent the night there to avoid walking in the middle of the day, and I ended up meeting an old friend from Battambang. This was an incredibly fortuitous encounter because my friend gave me 3 kilos (about 6 and one half pounds) of corn seed for my family back in the village.

The next morning, at sunrise, I hit the field, cutting back through the rice fields with water up to my waist. I carried nylon sacks on my back containing close to 50 pounds of rice and corn seed. It took some 12 hours, as every time I saw someone working, I changed direction so they would not spot me and turn me in. When I finally got onto dry land, I crawled on all fours to a tree and hung on for dear life. I was so hungry and tired, and my legs were numb from the pain of walking all day long. I could do nothing but rest for a while. I covered the backpack with banana leaves to make it look like I had been out in the woods gathering bananas all day. I sat for about 40 minutes as I gathered the strength to sneak back into the village. Once inside the village I made my way over to where our hut was and I gave all the rice and corn to my parents so they could separate them into smaller bags. They hurriedly hid the bags around the house. It had been a huge risk, but it had paid off. We had enough extra food to keep us going a little longer.

There were other ways to get a little extra food as well. During break time from planting rice, I foraged for wild vegetables, what the Chinese call *Ong Choy*, and brought these back to my parents. We put the *Ong Choy* in soups. Even with this extra food and nourishment, we were still so hungry at night that we often could not fall sleep. When we lay down, we could hear our stomach growling. So my nighttime excursions became a regular thing.

I knew full well that they would kill you for sneaking out, but when you are starving, you are not afraid of death.

When we weren't fighting hunger or exhaustion, we were fighting off disease. Malaria was a big problem in our area, and I eventually came down with it. It was a scorching 104 degrees outside, and I could not stop shaking. I was cold from head to toe. I could not work at all because I was so sick, and so they reduced my food allowance. Again my mother used her connections to find me some medicine. I do not know how she got the medicine because we had nothing to trade at this point. She must have talked to one of her friends into giving us what medicine they could spare. After a couple of weeks I recovered. I hated being sick because I was eating less but at least I had a break from the work.

When we had left Battambang, my father had managed to sneak out 200 ounces of gold with the family. Little by little, we traded the gold for food. We always cooked our extra rice in the water pot so the Khmer Rouge would not know we were cooking black-market food. And once the rice was cooked, we always fed the kids first and then the adults. After we fed the children, we would put them to sleep inside the mosquito net. We always ate after the children were asleep, but my little nephew never slept. He would sing "Mommy, Mommy, I am still hungry." We all felt badly for him because he always needed to eat more than the others and there just was never enough to go around. I remember we had to eat quickly to make sure the other children would not wake up and want to eat.

I have this picture in my mind of my little niece sitting in the doorway of the grain shed, slowly moving her hand in front of her face, trying to shoo the flies away, so skinny that you could count her ribs and see her hip bones sticking out, dying from starvation, yet never complaining, just slowly fanning the flies away, always missing the flies that were on her eyes and face. Her bony little body slowly painfully breathing as if even this simple act used up too much energy. Although I have forgotten many things, this image has stayed in my mind all these years. That image captures all the senseless cruelty of life during that time, when children were victims and parents were helpless.

After my father's gold ran out, my oldest brother, Tong Meng, traded a watch for 30 cans of rice. Since we had not eaten rice for a long time, we decided to cook the rice to create one solid meal instead of boiling it to make the thin rice soup we usually had. We gave a bowl to his starving son, hoping to ease his suffering, but after eating it, he got a stomach ache and died two days later. We think it had been so long since he had eaten a solid meal that his digestive system could not handle breaking down food anymore. My young niece, his older sister, sat there in her own pain, holding his little hand and stroking his forehead while he was dying. She watched her little brother take his last breath. He was only three years old and had known only the agony and pain of starvation in his short life. We buried him in an orange field nearby. To this day, we still cannot find where we buried him. Soon after that tragic blow, Tong Meng's youngest daughter also died. She was only one year old and starved to death as well. It hurt us beyond anything to see the little ones starve, to be helpless to stop their suffering. The only thing we could do is watch and cry on the inside.

Meanwhile, the rest of us had to carry on and try to survive. I remember sneaking out at night and chopping banana trees, so we could eat the heart of the tree or the bottom of the tree. We'd just eat the plain boiled tree heart. A couple of times, I went to a farm and found a baby papaya tree, which I chopped down. We'd boil and eat the insides, even though it often made us very sick.

I knew others in the village were suffering the same fate as our family was so I took it upon myself to teach a small group of young men in the village how to steal, and then we'd go out to see what we could find. We always stole from public farms, never from private farms, and never from the small plots of vegetables people grew around their living areas. We felt the vegetable farms on the public lands were fair game since that food was destined for the Khmer Rouge troops and village leaders. In the early evening, when people were no longer working in the fields, I would wait for a little darkness and go out into the fields and cut off pumpkins, winter melons or squash. We would only take enough for that night. That way, we could always come back the next night and steal more. When we got back to camp, we put the vegetables in the boiling pot, and we'd eat everything— peels, seeds, stems, and all— so the Khmer Rouge wouldn't find them. That meant when we ate a banana, we ate the peel as well. We couldn't leave a trace of anything.

Another way we found food was to go to the village's grain warehouse and scrape up leftover grains off the floor and try to find broken rice pieces. We then roasted whatever we found, smashed the grains with a rock, and ate the paste of boiled rice. Sometimes we boiled the rice grain powder, wrapped it in a banana leaf and grilled it over the fire. We got more and more creative as time passed, even going out to the field to trap and eat the rats. It's hard to believe, but if you caught a rat, you were considered very lucky. And even though I couldn't swim, I used to tie myself to a tree and swim down to the bottom of the river to look for fresh water clams. I knew I could drown, but I was so hungry that I didn't care. I am also very afraid of snakes, but one time, I saw a blue snake slide down a hole, so I dug down until I got hold of it. I skinned him out, made a fire and roasted him right there. No salt, no seasoning, nothing. It had been a long time since I had had any meat, and I remember thinking at the time that it was the best meat I had ever tasted.

We all looked forward to the rainy season because that meant we had more options fpr finding extra food. We could go down to a pond near the village and fish after work. This pond filled up with water and fish that came from the floods of the Tonle Sap, a big lake between Battambang province and Siem Reap that splits off from the Mekong River and floods huge swaths of land every year. We dragged nets through the water and gathered fish every day after work. We also found crab, field rats, water rats, and snakes, really, anything that moved and had flesh on it to eat. There were many of us who could no longer hold onto life and died while waiting for the rains to come.

Hunger compels a person to do anything to stop the pain of it. Hunger is also a fear that permeates your existence as you watch yourself gradually waste away, and in this situation, not be able to do anything to stop the slow march towards death. In fact, I no longer feared death because death was always lurking in the form of the Khmer Rouge. I became more concerned with the pain in my heart as I watched those I loved suffer the same decline. And in fact, many people simply did give up the will to live and resigned themselves to hunger and death. They no longer saw the point in living and just wanted to rid themselves of this life and allow their Buddhist beliefs to guide them to some better place. I watched many lose their minds under the pressure of constantly being watched and of not knowing who they could talk to or share an emotion. I knew that if I did not do something soon I was going to get like that as well.

To keep myself from going crazy I started a recipe book. It was my thinking if and when this phase of my life ever ended I could start a restaurant using all of the old recipes. I talked with elders in our village about their best recipes when I could find time. I had to be careful and ask them things very quickly and remember the recipe until I got back to our little hut. I could not be seen talking for too long with other villagers, as the leaders would think that we were plotting against them, but I managed to get the information I needed. I hid my recipe book below our little hut under a bit of burlap. I prayed to my ancestors no one of importance would find that book because it could have meant the end of my whole family. It sounds like a big risk, but this recipe book was a symbol of my hope this hell on earth would one day end. It represented a real future, one in which I could resume normal life, open a restaurant, and begin again.

You would have thought people would be inclined to help each other, but there was such an atmosphere of mistrust that people started to lash out at each other instead. We had to be very careful all the time. The village leader, Tuan, took a disliking to me because I had helped one of my fellow Chinese who was working with us. He fell very ill with a very bad headache and laid down on the ground. Everyone thought he was going to die, so I picked him up and carried him over a mile back to camp. Tuan yelled at me to stop carrying him and asked me why I was so concerned about him. Tuan kept yelling, "He is not a member of your group! Why are you helping him? Let him die." After I got back to the work site, the soldiers pulled me aside and told me to never do that again. I had to apologize and promise them I would not help anyone again. Tuan did not forget the episode and did his best to get back at me. Later the next day, Tuan gathered my family for a meeting. He claimed one of us had stolen someone else's vegetables. None of us had stolen anything, so I figured he was out to get me. That meant I had to be extra careful. When someone with Tuan's power did not like you, he could easily have talked to the people above him and made up all kinds of lies about me, and then it would be all over.

The constant threat of death took its toll on all of us. Over time, the regime transformed us into zombies, empty of any emotion or humanity. We covered our hearts and showed no kindness toward others. We spoke to no one we had not known before the Khmer Rouge and questioned even those we were closest to.

Over and over again, I saw people break down; they simply sat there and cried. Hope had left their hearts. Others stood up to the village leaders or soldiers in hopes of being killed. I somehow managed to retain a sense of myself by holding on to what little of the past I could. I saw my parents and treasured them. I looked at my cookbook from time to time and conjured memories of how I had felt cooking in my father's kitchen, bringing the smells of the food back to my consciousness and allowing that to flood my senses for a moment in time. I prayed hard to my ancestors for guidance and help in dealing with the daily onslaught. That is how I was able to withstand the pressure of living under the thumb of dictatorship.

MOVING ON

S everal weeks after the episode with the Chinese fellow in the field, Tuan, the village leader, was still after me, always giving me a hard time. I had a sense he wanted to get rid of me. I made the difficult decision to leave the village and my family. I had heard zone 3, an area near us, had more food and the leaders in that zone had more compassion for their workers. My parents were sad to see me go, partly because they were concerned for my well-being and partly because they were afraid no one would watch out for them. My older brothers were not around much because they were working in the forest, and my younger brothers were too young to be of much help. They wanted me to stay close to them so they could still have that sense of family.

I too felt sad and apprehensive about leaving. What if my leaving jeopardized the safety of my parents? What if the village leaders killed my whole family because I left? Would that make me feel selfish? I sat with my mother and father and talked it all through with them and they finally agreed I should go. I told my brothers to look after my parents and to watch out for themselves. One thing happened during this time that almost made me not leave my family. My one and only pair of shoes came up missing. Someone had stolen my old broken down pair of shoes. I used to watch after my shoes like a mother hen watches after her chicks. How far could I walk without shoes? And who would want to steal those things anyway? I began to wonder if this was someone's way of making sure that I stayed here in this village.

The next day I went to the cook during lunch break and asked for my share of rice. He said no, I had to wait for the whole group. So I just took off after that with nothing. No back pack, no extra clothes, not a single thing. (I heard later that the soldiers in Zone 4 came to my mother that night and asked about me. She said she did not know where I was. The soldiers told her, "If we ever catch him, we will kill him.") I crossed the river and walked 12 kilometers to the next village. I had to be careful to stay out of sight along the way. Soldiers patrolled the areas between villages and you had to have a permit to travel. Whenever I saw someone, I hid. I occasionally stopped to drink water out of the rice paddies or a nearby stream to try to stave off my hunger. Finally I came to the main road that separated areas. I cut across the fields and headed toward Anlong Run village.

I had almost completed my journey to zone 3 when I was captured by two *Chlubs* (spies). One of them was a couple of years older than me (about 24), while the other one looked to be only about twelve. They were carrying machetes and bayonets. They tied rope around my elbows and walked me through the village to the grain warehouse where the headquarters were. To make it even more painful, the soldiers tied the rope so tight that I felt like my chest muscles were going to rip or my ribs would break. The pain was so fierce that I broke out into a sweat. My elbows were almost touching each other behind my back, and I thought my shoulders were going to pop out of their sockets. Frankly, I have no idea why I didn't pass out from the pain. One of the soldiers put his knee in the middle of my back and pulled my shoulders even closer together. When I cried out in pain, he yelled at me to shut up or he would slit my throat and let me bleed out.

After that, I must have passed out for a while because I remember waking up in a grain warehouse. I discovered I was hanging with my hands over my head, the rope around my wrists, tied to the main beam. The rope was cutting into my wrists, and my arms felt like they were going to pop out of their sockets. I hung there for several hours until it got dark. All I know is that five minutes was far too long to hang this way and several hours in this position was almost unbearable. The soldiers started interrogating me and kept calling me a spy. I told them repeatedly I was no spy and I heard that the village leaders here were very nice. They ignored my replies and just kept asking me the same questions over and over again. The soldiers were so close to my face that I could smell their breath, see the veins in their foreheads popping out and smell the rancid sweat coming off them. They kept whacking me in the ribs to get me to confess I was a CIA spy. Every time I told them I was not a spy, the beatings started up again with increased ferocity. One attacked my ribs with a stick, while another beat the bottoms of my feet. I eventually blacked out from the pain, and then the torture would stop for a while. When I'd wake up, the cycle of questioning and beating would start again.

I finally managed to tell them my cousin's family lived in this village and that his wife was the head tailor for the village. They went and got her and she identified me. They cut me down and chained me to a pole by my right foot. They left me there all night long, while mosquitoes bit at me incessantly. They did not give me anything but water all night. The next morning, the door opened up and there were two new soldiers standing there. One had a gun and the other a machete. They unlocked the chain from my leg and tied me back up again around the elbows. The one with the machete stuck his knee into my back so hard that my chest bones and muscles started to pop and snap.

They put me on a dog leash and told me to start walking down the main road out of the village. I was very nervous because the guards were right behind me with their guns at the back of my head. I knew if I did not do exactly as they said, they would shoot me in the back of the head. As I started down the road, I heard a shot come whizzing past me. Then I heard them tell me to turn right towards the bushes. Normally, the Khmer Rouge killed people in the bushes. So I figured I was done for. I did as I was told, my heart beating out of my chest with terror. The guards were still right behind me with their guns aimed right at me, so I just kept on going. We walked through the bush for quite a ways and all the time I kept expecting them to shoot me in the head. We walked and walked for what seemed quite a long time. I managed to look up to the sun and was able to tell it was around noon.

While walking, I started to pray to my grandmother. She told me when I was young that whenever I was in trouble, just pray for her and she would come and help me. I prayed to her and asked her, "Where are you now Grandma? I need you badly! Please help me now! Help me!!" As soon as I stopped my prayers I looked off and up to my right and saw a big grass hut in the woods and a group of soldiers inside. I had heard of this place from the whispers of people whose relatives had disappeared. This was where they chopped people up and got rid of the bodies. If the rumors were true, they hit you in the head, split you open, took out your liver and ate it, usually raw.

Once we got to the hut, the interrogation began anew. I told them what I had told the other soldiers, I had heard that the village leaders here were good and nice people and there was food. Again they asked me if I was a spy, and again I told them "no I was just a hard worker who wanted more food." Whenever they would ask me something, I acted crazy and kept smiling at them. Inside I was scared out of my mind, afraid that I was going to die at any moment. I'd heard the Khmer Rouge killed all the smart ones but not the crazy ones. So I figured acting crazy might keep me alive—and it seemed to be working so far.

The soldiers chained me back up by my leg and tied me to the pole of the grass hut. It was pouring down rain, and I slept there on the ground, fending off mosquitoes all night long. Whenever I had to go to the bathroom, they lengthened the chain and held an AK-47 on me so I could not run away. I considered myself lucky, as I was still alive and the torture had stopped. When I woke up, I continued to play along with acting crazy. I flattered them with comments like, "You are so good and your leadership of the village is good." I would ask them for mercy.

I would drop down on both knees, dropping my head to the ground in a prayerful way, acting like they were some sort of god.

The second day, around noon I think, they gave me a full plate of rice and some vegetable soup. I had not eaten that much rice in a long time, and the soup was hot and flavorful. I felt much better after that. While I was eating, another soldier rode up on a motorcycle carrying a .45 caliber handgun. These were the people that called the shots. He yelled to the other soldiers, "Where did this one come from? Kill him now!" I was so shocked and afraid that I stopped eating. The rice starting spilling out of my mouth, and I could not get my hands to stop shaking. The only thought that came across my mind was, "Well, at least if they kill me now, I will not be a hungry ghost!"

Again, luck prevailed. The soldier on the motorcycle drove away and the soldiers did not kill me. Around 5:00 p.m. (I am guessing based on where the sun was in the sky), I was given a bowl of rice. I bowed down to the soldiers the way we used to when we prayed to Buddha. I got on my knees with my legs behind me and put my hands to my face and told the soldiers, "Thank you for saving my life. You are so wonderful for saving my life. I bless you, I bless you." I was saying these things in hopes they would not kill me. I knew the Khmer Rouge liked to kill people at night, so when darkness fell, I slept with one eye open, just in case they came for me. I was so nervous I woke up at the smallest sound, even the wind blowing through the trees. When the sun rose on the third day, I said to myself, "I am alive for another day. Maybe I can make it one more day." They began to interrogate me once again, and I told them I was from the village run by Uncle Wung. Uncle Wung was a Khmer Rouge who had been kind to the people in his village. Unlike so many others, he had a soft heart and had been good to me because I was a good worker and willing to help people out.

The soldiers sent one of their compatriots out to Wat Ga Go to check on my story. I hoped if they asked Uncle Wung about me, they would learn that I was a good worker and they would accept me into this village. I sat and waited as patiently I could for food. In fact, the best thing about being in captivity was eating real food again. I was fed twice a day, and when I got done eating, they actually asked me if I was full and got me more rice! I was starting to relax a tiny bit around these soldiers and I stopped fearing for my life.

On the fourth day, the soldiers who had left returned to the camp and start talking amongst each other. I could not hear what they were talking about and did not want to guess either. I stayed in the camp all day long, and only had to go through some lighter interrogation this time. On the fifth day, they suddenly let me go, telling me I could stay in Anlong Run. I found out later the two soldiers did go and check out my story and Uncle Wung had indeed told them I was a good person and a hard worker. This is what saved my life. I think it must have been the prayer to my grandmother that kept me alive through this ordeal. I was near tears after they released me. I felt as though a huge weight was lifted from my shoulders, and I was a free man, even if that feeling was only fleeting. As soon as I got out of the bushes I raised my arms like I was flying. I felt so happy and relieved and I got out of there as quickly as I could and walked unaccompanied into Anlong Run.

When I arrived, I came across several people from Battambang. I knew them from my father's restaurant, and they were very happy to see me. They told me I was very lucky to come back because just last month, a former classmate had run off like I did and had never returned. No one ever knew what happened to him. Everyone assumed he was killed. In my heart I said a prayer to my grandmother to thank her for her protection. I laid out all my feelings to her and even shed a few tears of thanks after the ordeal was over. I turned back to the reality before me and hid my soft heart away.

The local Khmer Rouge gave me a grass hut to live in. I had no blankets or rug or anything, so I just lay down on the bamboo rack. I was emotionally drained from my five days of captivity, and my head was swirling from all I had been through. What pulled me out of this state of mind was the ever-present sting of the mosquitoes. I started a small fire underneath my rack to smoke them out. Once the fire started and the mosquitoes flew off, I fell fast asleep. I slept like I had not slept in years. It was a deep, full sleep during which I dreamed about the past, when we were all back at home, working our restaurant and living our normal lives. But my dream was a short lived reprieve from reality, as morning dawned and I was going to have to find out what was in store for me at Anlong Run.

First thing, I went to a meeting with the village leader and told him I was married, but that I had lost track of where my wife was. Saying this would put me in the family group, where I would not have to work as hard as in the young man's group. I was able to work around the village, cooking and doing repairs

father's failing health really worried us, but there was nothing we could do.

People in the village liked me because I always helped out with whatever I could. They put me to work with the person who was in charge of the 30-family group. I was hoping that being in a position like this would be more beneficial for my family in that we could get more food or maybe not have to work as hard. Being the assistant to the group leader allowed me to work directly with others in the village. Soon people began to trust me and felt comfortable talking with me because they knew I would not tell my superiors about anything bad that was said about either village leaders or Angkar. This enabled me to be a voice for the villagers. There were complaints from the villagers about treatment and I soon realized that I was powerless to institute any change but I still listened to everyone's issues. I think it made everyone feel better.

Each section in a village consisted of 30 families, and one person was in charge of the group. The head person then had three people underneath them, and then each of those three had three others beneath them. The last three were each assigned to watch 10 families. If any one of the families or people watching the families had problems or did not report on the families that were in their command, the area executioner would come in and chop off the whole branch. That is how the Khmer Rouge ruled the villages and camps. There was always somebody watching someone all of the time. Any deviation from that was a sure death for all involved. It was nothing for them to come in and kill one hundred people in a family and the people who were supposed to be managing that family.

I never knew why things in Anlong Run were easier for us than in other areas I had been in. It could have been the upper managers of the area had ties to the Khmer Rouge leadership. It could have been something as simple as someone being married to a niece or a sister of someone in the leadership. We never learned why Anlong Run had food and eight kilometers away people were starving to death. I used to think it was part of some wicked master plan, like a grim version of chess, in which the Khmer Rouge leadership tried to see which area would die off faster. It is just a crazy guess, but late at night I used to think about all this until it literally almost drove me crazy.

One day, we were digging down a divider between rice fields and I got bitten by a poisonous black centipede. My whole right side turned red with poison, and I immediately fell down and started to swell up. I felt a chill across my body, and despite the heat, I suddenly had teeth-rattling chills. I could not hold my jaw or my body still. The violent shakes drained me of what little energy I had.

What saved my life was an older person in the village who knew about ancient medicine. He gathered some bark and leaves off of a tree, boiled them down and put the mixture on my leg. It helped the infection somewhat, but the bite itself remained really swollen and infected. Where the centipede bit me, there were two holes in my foot about one centimeter in size. Since I had no shoes, the rice shafts would pierce those holes again and again, sending pain shooting through my body like an electric shock. I thought I might die from the pain. At one point, a fly landed on the open wound and crawled up into the infected hole. I could feel the fly moving around in my leg, but I couldn't do anything. I could not scratch the fly out. I could not pull the fly out; I could only wait for the fly to crawl back out of the hole. Finally, days later, the fly emerged and flew away. I do not know how long the fly was up in there, but I can tell you that every day was hell.

Right after I recovered from my infection my third brother, Kheang, became quite ill, so ill that they had to put him in a hospital. Well, it wasn't really a hospital since the Khmer Rouge had shut all the hospitals down, but it was a sort of public clinic. The patients brought their own hammocks, tied them off on the posts, and used those as their sick beds. They laid and waited to be administered some homemade herbal medicine. It was not really medicine but something the Khmer Rouge had concocted to make people think they were actually getting medicine. Most likely, it was just coconut juice.

My brother was in the hospital during one of the Cambodian holidays, and one of the so-called "nurses" had brought some sweet rice wrapped in banana leaves with mung beans inside, a traditional holiday treat the Cambodians call *Nam-a-som*. We had left our brother and had gone back home to rest. We were all asleep when all of a sudden I woke up and saw my brother sneak into our house. He had somehow managed to steal two of these treats for our family. He had wrapped them up in his *gama* (the Cambodian neckerchief), and he opened it in front of me, and they were still steaming hot and looked delicious. I woke my parents up and we devoured them like we were children doing something really naughty. When we were done, my brother went out into the woods and buried the banana leaves.

He crossed in and out of the shadows of the moonlit night, hoping and praying to our ancestors that he would not get caught. He was very fortunate to make it back to the hospital unnoticed. He had not been missed at all. It was a memorable night. The dessert managed, for a short time, to ease our anguish and bring back memories of a better time. It was small pleasures such as these that kept us going.

BACK TO WORK

During rice planting season the Khmer Rouge needed people to go work in the rice field called Rung Drea, about 40 kilometers from Anlong Run. We were there to plant what is called short-term rice, which grows in just three and a half months.

Here's how it works, before the rainy season, the rice seed is thrown out into the fields. The rice sits there until the rains come, at which point the seeds take root in the mud and water and the rice grows to the level of the flood. The rice can be as high as 2 meters, and the rice grains grow on the surface. As the rice paddy grows, the plants are pushed closer together. Once they reach a certain height, they are transplanted to the paddy fields, where they mature. Transplanting the rice plants is painful, back-breaking work, during which you spend up to ten hours a day bent over. After gathering up the plants, we carried the bundles of rice plants across several acres, and then doubled over to drop the plants in one smooth motion. We pushed a hole in the ground with our thumbs, pushed in a few plants, then moved on to the next hole, and the next, until row upon row of rice was planted, and sprouts of green formed neat lines across the field. Once transplanted, we weeded and tended to the plants.

Although we were occasionally rotated out for other assignments, we generally stayed in Rung Drea for three months at a time, endlessly working the rice.

More and more people came to work at Rung Drea, and there was only one cook for all of them. One of the old men started to ask around for another cook, so I went to the person in charge and told him I could do some things in the kitchen. I begged him to let me cook, and he agreed to give me a chance. I began to assist with the cooking and the cleaning. Working in the kitchen was much easier than toiling away in the fields. I was able to eat a little more and started to recover from starvation. It was a relatively good period while it lasted.

Unfortunately, that phase ended, and I was sent out on a variety of other work projects which tested my endurance and patience. I got my feet cut up when I had to go cut elephant grass (whose leaves have razor-sharp edges) without any shoes. I learned to climb tall bamboo trees, cut them down, and float them down the river, fending off leeches and dangerous monitor lizards. My group was sent out to split the rocks for a dam. My hands split open from cracking the rocks, and I had painful blisters that bled. Sometimes I could not even open my hands up, but I had to keep on working. After splitting the rocks, we put them up on our shoulders and carried them down to the river bottom and then mixed and poured concrete to make the foundation for the dam. We formed lines that started where the cement was mixed and passed the buckets of cement from person to person, hand to hand and poured out until the cement was gone. This went on around the clock for thirty hours. Everyone was exhausted to the point of passing out. I finally took a break and leaned against an orange tree and was so tired I fell asleep standing up. My hands had to be closed because if opened totally up the calluses would open and would start to bleed. My knees were swollen and stiff from working on my knees to spread out the concrete. I had never thought of myself as a slave to the Khmer Rouge but my mind was beginning to understand the slave mentality.

The sun burned down on us, sucking all the life out, to the point where you felt you could not go on and death would be a welcome escape. You had to tell yourself maybe there was going to be an end to all of this pain, try to figure out a reason why any person would allow this to happen to another person. Why did we, the people of Cambodia, deserve all of this pain and suffering? Would it ever stop? No one knew if there would be a tomorrow. Every day the same thing, mindless back breaking painful work. I can remember times where the sun would blister the skin on my back through holes of my little black jacket. I would come home at night and stitch the tear closed with long grass that I would wrap tightly together and use as thread. The hole would be covered up and would last a couple of days. The leeches in the field were another problem altogether.

There were times when we had to stop planting rice and take time to pull off the leeches because we could no longer stand the pain of hundreds of leeches putting their hooks in us. We had to be extra careful because the leeches left behind a little poison where they attached themselves which would cause serious infections if left alone. We had to be careful to not be seen by the soldiers because the Khmer Rouge would see you stop and beat you for being lazy.

In the fall of 1977, I got assigned to work in the grains warehouse. I used to sneak my way into the warehouse by climbing over the wall and take yams or mung beans or rice grains for my father to eat for that day. I was worried about his health because his health seemed to be going down hill. I sometimes had to carry one hundred fifty pound bags of rice into the warehouse every day and it amazed me that we were producing so much rice, yet we were starving. While there, I ran into a fortune teller. I recognized him as the one who used to sit in the Battambang market near my parents' restaurant. He said to me, "Hey, after lunch come by my house and visit me." I went to his hut and sat down, and he said to me, "Give me your hand." He asked me what year I was born. I told him the date and he started to draw a dragon. The old man told me this was called dragon bone counting. As he drew, he said to me, "I do not know if you believe me or not but bring a notebook and write down what I tell you. If what I tell you does not come true, you come and find me." I was very intrigued and asked him to please continue with my fortune.

He told me when I was born there was something with me, some spirit that can drive a person crazy, but that I was very smart, slick, and aggressive. He told me if I traveled somewhere this month, I should be very careful because I might lose something. (In the same month, they sent me into the woods to chop down trees and I lost my backpack, which contained pretty much everything I owned at the time. I remembered what the old man said and realized his prediction had come true.)

The fortune teller also told me, "In your lifetime, sometimes you worry about having something to eat tomorrow, but someone will bring you food that night; sometimes you worry about things, but you always get through. This is how your life is. It is that spirit which is helping you out, looking out for you." He told me I would get married when I was 24 (I was 22 at the time), I did not know the girl yet but she was meant to be my wife and she will be smaller and light in complexion and that it does not matter what happens in life you are destined to grow old together. He said when I turned thirty-three I would be a boss or own my own business and that I would be a successful businessman. And if I was going to be a soldier I would be the general.

He also said the further west I went, the better my life would be. He said when I got there, I needed to settle down and change my name and this would change my luck. Doing those things would give me much success. While he spoke, I must confess I didn't believe much of what he said. It all seemed a little farfetched to me. How was someone going to know what was going to happen to me years from now? However, the village elders all said that he was a great fortune teller and what he predicted would come true. Consumed by getting through the present, I promptly forgot all about it, though I would remember his words years later.

Gradually, very, very gradually, life got a little easier. The village leaders trusted me because they saw I was willing to do any work that was assigned, and they let me come and go from the village. Since I had been out in the forest many times, I knew where bamboo was and where the hardwood trees were.

I made connections up in the forest with the small farmers in the area and would chop trees or bamboo down for them and trade for tobacco, fruit or vegetables and return to the village and give what I brought back to the village leaders. I was looked upon favorably for these actions and won favor with the leaders. When I worked along the Bavel River, I managed to steal fruit, which gave me strength and restored my spirits a bit. It felt good to eat something besides watered-down rice soup. In fact, I can still taste the fruit today in my mind.

MY FATHER

While we were being starved and worked to death, my father was slowly dying. We did not know what he was dying from because there was no medical care, but we could see that he had a growth on his neck and figured that was what was making him sick. I can only assume that it was some form of cancer. He couldn't work, so he just sat in the house, moaning in pain. He used to look up to heaven and ask why this was happening to him. "Why me? After all I have done to help others, why me?" My father had spent his whole life taking care of others in our community, looking after the aged, making sure they had food and money for emergencies. He took better care of others than he did of himself. We all felt the injustice of it deeply.

Whenever we returned to the village after our work projects, we took turns rubbing his shoulders or wiping his brow, and talked with him, trying to ease his mind and distract him from the pain. I was furious at the Khmer Rouge for refusing to help him in his final days. My mother worried all the time, as she knew that this sickness was going to end with her losing her husband. She felt powerless as she watched the life draining out of both of them, just as the Khmer Rouge was draining the spirit out of our family and country.

By now, it was 1978, and I found myself working on the dam at Ta Haen, which was in the mountains far away from the village. When it came time for me to go home for my monthly visit, I walked the whole day to get home. I saw right away that my father looked extremely bad, and it seemed clear that death was imminent. I did whatever I could to ease his suffering. Sometimes he tried to say something to me and I had to get up right next to his mouth to hear him. But every time he tried to talk, he coughed a cough that racked his whole body and moaned in pain. I would force the tears and pain back into my heart. For some reason, I needed my father to see me as a strong man. I did not know it at the time, but that one day with him would be the last time I saw my father alive. The next day, I had to walk back to camp. A couple of weeks after I returned, my brother, Kok Kheng, who was up at the dam with me, got permission to go the village to check on our father. When Kheng returned, he told me that I should go see him because the end was near. My brother Kheang had been in the mountains working, he had heard from the villagers that my father had passed away so.

I went to the leader of the construction site and told them that my father had died. I asked him for permission to go back to the village. He casually replied, "Well, people die all the time. Why do you want to go? If you go, your father will not come back, so what the hell you want to go for?" I was so angry that I lashed back: "To hell with you. I am going back. Do you want to kill me? You can do it when I get back." I called their bluff and started on the trek home with my brother.

As we approached our hut in the village, I started to cry because I could not see my father inside. I screamed at the heavens, "Why did you take my father? Why not take some of the evil people?" When we got inside, we asked our brother Heng what, if anything, were our father's last words. He said to us "Father's last breath was spent telling me he wanted us to protect Chai and make sure he gets an education so he can become whatever he wants." Heng then told us that when my father died, my mother just sat in a daze, with a look on her face that showed she had no idea what to do. My mother was a very strong woman who used to make all the big decisions in the family, but this time, she was at a loss. And it really scared us to see her sitting there in total silence, a broken shell of a woman. She looked as though she could stand no more of this insanity. We could see in her eyes all the pain she had held inside. She allowed no one to come close to her. It seemed she wanted to wallow in the darkness of the loss of her husband, and let herself be swept away by the waves of sadness.

My Father's reburial service

My father was buried in his only T-shirt and pants, then in a rice sack since we could not sacrifice our few blankets, which my mom needed to sleep in at night. (Much later, in the late 80's, my uncle and my brothers Kheang and Kheng found my father and moved his remains to a Buddhist temple in Battambang. They got a coffin and had a funeral ceremony. Those members of our family who were still in Cambodia put him to rest properly, far from the insanity of the Khmer Rouge. It is good to know that he is now at peace.)

THE BEGINNING OF THE END

Finally, in late 1978, we began to see the end of the Khmer Rouge. Throughout the Khmer Rouge regime, I never saw any trains. Then suddenly, there was a lot of truck traffic in the area and trains coming and going. At first, we couldn't figure out what the increase in traffic was about, but then we heard through the grapevine that the Vietnamese had invaded the country near the Vietnamese border. It became obvious to me that the Khmer Rouge were sending supplies and troops into that area to fight the Vietnamese. Later, we saw troop movements on the road heading towards Phonm Penh, which confirmed our suspicions. Several people approached the troops and asked them where they were heading, but the soldiers simply drew their weapons and shot anyone who spoke to them.

During our time in Anlong Run, a man named Brother Moan was our group leader. Although he was a Khmer Rouge, he was not connected with their military faction. More of an administrator than anything, he was not like the rest of the Khmer Rouge. He was kind and actually worked with us in the village to make life somewhat easier. Even though he was a native Cambodian, he resisted the Khmer Rouge's racially charged notion that they had to get rid of their "Chinese" problem. There was a lot of pressure on Brother Moan because his superiors knew that change was in the air. They were pressing him to get rid of the "traitors" in their midst. We'd survived up to this point, and we didn't want to disappear when there was finally a ray of hope.

Then we heard more rumors of fighting along the border of Vietnam and that the Khmer Rouge had engaged the Vietnamese army and was taking a beating. We all wanted to know what was going on, so I went to Brother Moan's wife and asked her if we could listen to their radio. I had to ask her in such a way that she would not think I was a traitor. I said very carefully, "Sister Moan, please let us listen to the radio, so we can prepare ourselves against our enemy," implying that the enemy was the Vietnamese, of course. She agreed, and that's when we realized that change was definitely coming soon. We did not know how long it would take the Vietnamese forces to free us, but we now knew that we would be freed from this hell on earth. Of course we could not show our joy at the news that the Khmer Rouge armies were getting beaten down. Some of us took a chance and snuck out to the woods to discuss the news and the changes that were coming. Some spoke at night in whispered tones in their little huts. It was all whispers here, sneaking a chat there, but soon the entire village was abuzz with the news.

Brother and Sister Moan had pretended to be loyal to the Khmer Rouge, but then the Khmer Rouge dug deeper into Brother Moan's past. It turns out that he had hidden his past well but not as well as he thought. Some of his relatives had been school teachers in the old government, while others had been important figures in the old Cambodian army. This meant that both Brother and Sister were suddenly slated to be "disposed of." They left soon after and headed for Thailand as quickly as possible. They got out by the skin of their teeth as the Khmer Rouge army chased their little family all the way to the border, shooting at them until they crossed into Thailand.

It's worth jumping ahead here to say that, years later, our paths crossed again. Through some six degrees of separation, I contacted a friend of mine from that period who told me that he knew Brother Moan and he lived near Olympia, just south of Seattle. I called Brother Moan up and told him I held nothing against him; I realized he was in a tough spot and that he did what he had to do. He was a part of something that he had no control over, and if he had not done as he was told, it would have meant the end of him and his family. I reassured him that I held no ill will towards him and that he was a good man caught in a bad situation. I told him that I still remembered that he had gone out of his way to treat us with respect and kindness. He thanked me and told me that my words validated his feelings that he was doing the right thing for the people in his care.

Even before the Khmer Rouge the Chinese in the country were treated somewhat separately but "equal". At the age of sixteen I went to sign up for the army and was told that I could not join since I was not ethnically Cambodian. Even though I was born in the country and I thought of that country as my homeland, even though I spoke fluent Cambodian and we had a business that catered to and hired Cambodians we were not considered true Cambodian. Our ID card for the country said Chinese on it. Nowhere did it say Cambodian. It just said

Chinese. It was the government's way of saying that we were not the same as the Cambodians. That was something that I had a hard time with when I was that age. I truly felt that my family was Cambodian.

Despite the rumblings of change, our life remained the same for quite some time. We still worked all the time, and, in fact, life actually became *more* dangerous for awhile. We had to be even more vigilant about what we said and who we spoke to. We had to make sure that the soldiers in the area did not hear us breathe a word about the war. We were not supposed to know about such things, and revealing that we had any knowledge at all would most certainly have been the end for us.

Curiously, in January 1979 I saw two trains running down the train tracks, one after the other, and I took them as a sign that we would be free soon. I wanted to be prepared, so I went and found a machete, some axes, a knife and rope, anything I thought that I could use in case all hell broke loose. I hid my weapons in the straw underneath my hammock, figuring they might come in handy and may even save my life.

A week after this, several Khmer Rouge soldiers came through our village. I got up my nerve and approached them, asking them as politely as I could, "Where are you going?" They said nothing in return. They just moved through, heading rapidly west to the Thai border. I assumed that they were getting out of the area because the Vietnamese had invaded and that this meant the Khmer Rouge were on the run. I could feel that freedom was near.

The Khmer Rouge started calling for five people who took care of the oxen and the ox carts, wanting to load up everything they could: guns, extra bullets, food, and whatever else they could find. I decided to volunteer to help with the carts because I was curious about what was going on. I told my mother that I had been called into service, and she just told me to watch my back, to come back home, and help out the family. I told her not to worry. What the soldiers did not know was that I used someone else's ox and ox cart and left my cart with my family, so that they could start getting ready to go.

I had an instinct as we walked toward the community center that after we helped them load up their stuff, they would kill us or force us to go with them. So I told the others to leave as soon as they were done. I ran into the village leader on my way out, who told me to go back and make sure that all the supplies are in order, but I got the hell out of there with my group.

When I got back to the village, I took out the weapons that I had hidden away, sharpened them to a fine edge, and gave them to my brothers. I told my brothers that I was going to kill someone that night. I was looking for a person whose name was Huan. He had mistreated us for a long time, and I felt the need to get my revenge. I knew that this was my chance to kill him because of all the chaos all around us—no one would even notice. I went out to look for him, yelling his name at the top of my lungs. I yelled out in the middle of the night like a dog howling at the moon. Huan heard his name, and he knew that I was coming to seek vengeance. I searched high and low, but I could not find this man.

After several hours of searching, I gave up, went home and started to get ready to leave the area. Everyone was getting ready to leave, but the problem was that no one knew where to go, which direction was safe. I told them that we needed to head back to the cities because if we headed west, we would be walking toward the fighting, toward the Khmer Rouge, and that we could end up walking into a trap or face more torture. There were no real leaders at this point, so I took charge by starting to tell people to head east; In the middle of the night I got my family together, (Me, my mother, Kok Heng, Chai, Kok Kheng and Tong Meng) gathered up what supplies we could find. I sent my family ahead of me and I stayed a little behind to make sure that no one would follow them and attack them and take the meager supplies they had. They started to walk east towards the main road towards Battambang which was about 12 kilometers away cutting across the fields. From the fields they got on to one of the highways that split Battambang province. The main road was filled with people on the move, heading back to either their home villages or into Battambang. There was not a single Khmer Rouge soldier anywhere. We figured that most or all of them had gotten out of the country through Thailand just ahead of the Vietnamese Army. It hadn't taken them long to make themselves scarce.

Strange as it may sound, we didn't even have time to rejoice or think about our newfound freedom. We did not even really dare believe that we were really and truly free. It still seemed like it could be part of a massive trick, like they would get us all out onto the main road just to gun us down. The overall atmosphere was one of widespread chaos and confusion. No one knew what was going on. My only thought was to get back into town and to try and find somewhere to settle down, find some food and some safety, and then see what happened next. Trying to grasp the rapid change of events really threw me into a state of confusion. One day we were under the thumb of the Khmer Rouge, working away as hard as we could and slowly starving to death. The next day, we were out on our own, with no real idea of what was going to happen to us and the country. Although we hated the Khmer Rouge, we at least more or less understood the rules of the game at that point—we still felt marginally safe if we did what we were told. Now, we were facing the great unknown. I felt like a chicken jumping from the boiling pot into the frying pan. But for now, we walked until we got to Wat Ga Go where we stayed for several days.

The very next day, as we continued along the highway into the city, we ran right into the Vietnamese Army. They were patrolling the road into Battambang, making it safe for people to get into town. The Vietnamese Army was afraid that there was still a large Khmer Rouge contingency in the area and did not want a slaughter on their hands. The army personnel were very friendly with me because I spoke to them in Vietnamese. They wanted to know where I was heading. When I told them I was going back into my hometown of Battambang, they wished me good luck and I went on my way. We viewed the Vietnamese as our liberators and were grateful beyond words for their intervention on our behalf.

As we walked, we witnessed mayhem breaking out all around. We saw people grabbing pigs and rice, looting and stealing whatever they could get their hands on. I was with a friend out foraging for food, when we saw two young Khmer

Rouge soldiers with AK47s at the ready. I yelled to them, "Come over here and I will chop your heads off!" All of a sudden, I heard bullets whizzing past us. We cleared out of there and returned to the main road and headed back towards Wat Ga Go. When we got back to where my family was waiting I went to my mother and saw that she had been crying. One of her friends had come by and told her that someone had seen me get shot in the forehead. I gave her a big hug and told her that it was not me who was shot but it was a friend of mine. Unfortunately, my friend had been married only one month when he was killed by one of the Khmer Rouge. We settled everyone down for the night and tried to get some sleep but there were a lot of things going on all around us. People were up talking and yelling with the sounds of people fighting mixed in. I remember that no one slept very comfortably that night. I slept with one eye open and a hand on my machete in case anyone tried to attack us.

The following day came too soon and with it came some issues with four of the villagers from Anlong Run. I was trying to get a fire going to cook some food and they came over to me and demanded that I give them my cow, claiming that I had stolen it from them. I told them that I had been using that cow for over a year and I knew it was mine. They started circling around me, grabbed the rope from me, and starting pulling the cow down the street. My anger exploded, so I grabbed my axes and chased them down the road and told them that I would kill all of them if they did not give me back my cow. I must have scared them badly because they immediately let me take the cow back.

During this time, it was acceptable to carry a machete and axe, so most people had some sort of protection with them at all times. Right after the Khmer Rouge fell all the normal rules just fell apart. It was everyone out for themselves, without any regard for societal norms or common decency. People were so desperate and so volatile after being repressed for so long that they just lashed out without reason. Cambodian society had effectively fallen apart. As I fought to defend what little we had and to look after my own family, I pondered the cruel injustice that life after the Khmer Rouge seemed to be even more dangerous and unpredictable than when they were in power.

Early the next morning, I had to go out and look for food. While I was away, my brother, Kok Kheang, arrived. He had walked out of the woods up in the mountains where he had been chopping wood and making lumber. He had not been in our area very long when he got jumped by several people and they stole his cow and wagon. When I got back from foraging for food, my mother told me how he'd been beaten and robbed. I was furious and wanted to find the people who were responsible. How dare they steal from us when we had nothing? My mother calmed me down and told me wisely, "No, do nothing. Let them have the cow. It is far better to not cause any problems right now. We are lucky to still be alive and together as family." It took a while for me to calm down though. After having to hide my anger and resentment all these years, my rage was finally surfacing and could no longer be contained. I wanted to exact revenge in any way I could.

After the Khmer Rouge evaporated in thin air, there was a power vacuum that was filled by the Vietnamese Army.

The army leaders quickly imposed martial law. This may sound like a bad thing, but before they took over, no laws were being enforced at all, and some quite vicious murders took place as a result of lack of food. A curfew was imposed, and no one was allowed on the streets after 8:00 p.m. Check points were put into place to stem the flow of Khmer Rouge back in the area. The Vietnamese Army didn't want them to come back and make trouble. When they found little pockets of Khmer Rouge, they executed them on the spot.

There was nothing to buy or sell, and we were all still wearing our Khmer Rouge issued uniforms, which were starting to smell because we had not washed them in quite some time. To get food, we had to leave the village and head out to the countryside to rob farms or find fruit trees that had not yet been picked over. Huge numbers of people were in transit, moving out of the countryside and clogging the main roads. Most of us were in shock that the Khmer Rouge, who had been invincible for so long, had fallen apart so fast. Many walked around asking about relatives and loved ones, hoping with all their hearts that they could find a familiar face and find comfort in their arms.

My brother, Kok Kheang, decided to return right away to Battambang. He had heard from friends that his wife and her family had left the village that they were in and made it safely back into the city. We found out later that he found his wife and that most of her family had survived. We were still missing our sister at this point, but finally heard through my second brother's widow that she was in a village 40 kilometers away living there with her son.

HOME AGAIN: PUTTING OUR LIVES BACK TOGETHER

O n our third night in Wat Ga Go, we had a brief family meeting and decided the best thing to do would be to return to Battambang and see what was left of our life there. So the next day, we started the journey back to the house that my father had built for the family.

There was a palpable fear that accompanied us on our trip because none of us knew what kind of situation we were walking into. Even though the trip was rather short there was no guarantee that we would not be attacked along the way. I walked with my eyes wide open and my body tensed and ready for anything. I had the younger and older family members walk surrounded by stronger ones. That way, in case of attack, the men could respond and protect them.

When we arrived, it was good to see that the house was still standing. But as I knew from when I'd snuck back years before, all of our furniture, including some beautiful teakwood and ironwood pieces, had been taken. All around us, people were moving back into the city and hoping to return to their old homes. Some people arrived only to find that someone had already claimed their house.

Since all of the paperwork on ownership had disappeared, it was extremely difficult, if not impossible, to prove ownership. The public market started up again soon after we arrived, but not in the same place as before. People used gold and rice as currency instead of money. You could trade one 14 ounce can of rice for vegetables for dinner. If you wanted to buy a bike, you used gold.

As we looked around the city we saw others in our situation. Many had come back into the city looking for some semblance of their former lives only to find even more disappointment. The schools had been torn down, the public market, where our restaurant had been, was no longer standing. Amazingly none of the temples around Battambang had been damaged. Even one of the biggest Buddha's had been bombed but suffered no damage. Many in the city saw that as a good sign.

A few days after we'd come home, our sister arrived on the doorstep and found us in the old house. She had her two year old son with her, who was so emaciated from starvation that we did not recognize him. His eyes were popping out of his head, the skin was hanging off him, and his stomach was extremely bloated from malnutrition. His shoulder bones were sticking out and we could count all of his ribs. My sister said he was sick all the time and would not talk. We asked her where her husband was, and, very slowly, she told us between tears that he had died while out on a job chopping trees for the Khmer Rouge. All the Khmer Rouge told her was that he got sick and died. My sister started to cry so hard that she had a hard time even catching her breath between sobs. We held her up so she would not collapse on the floor, and when we grabbed her, we realized that she was nothing but skin and bones as well.

I had never seen my sister in this kind of emotional turmoil. Her chest was heaving between sobs and the tears were flowing like rivers across her bony face and down onto our arms. We all embraced her, but even that comfort was not enough to stop her pain. She kept yelling out to the heavens, "They killed my husband! They killed him." She eventually calmed down enough to sleep. We made some rice to feed to the baby, mashing it into porridge because his body couldn't handle solid foods, and fed him bits of mango that we had foraged.

Then my cousin and her son showed up. My cousin's husband and six of her seven children had died under the Khmer Rouge. She just cried and cried over her losses, and there was not a thing we could do to make any of it less painful. One of the daughters had been killed because another member of her group had killed a Khmer Rouge soldier. The others had starved. At the end, her children did not even have enough strength to bury their own father. Hard as it may be to believe, we all eventually became kind of numb to these kinds of stories. We had heard so much about pain and death that they barely fazed us anymore. We obviously felt for everyone around us who had lost family, and we mourned our own losses, but we also felt desperate to move forward, to leave the past behind, to get our lives started again.

Every day while we were in Battambang, my brothers and I had to go in search of food. We always left the city and went up the Sangker River way out behind the Vietnamese front line. We always had to be extra careful because there was still some Khmer Rouge away from the city and if the Khmer Rouge found us they would kill us just as soon as look at us. Some days we were lucky enough to find a chicken, maybe a small pig, or some fresh vegetables or fruit, but we grabbed anything remotely usable or edible. We made a lot of soup to stretch the food as far as possible. Sometimes, we went searching together, and other times, we would all split up. Our nephew (the one who lost all of his family except his mother) wanted to help out, but we wanted him to stay safe and close to his mother, so we gave him little jobs close to home.

Unfortunately, we could no longer stay at our house. With the fall of the Khmer Rouge came the rise of the Cambodian regular army who was assisting the newly established government. The army was being used in a variety of ways so when the Cambodian army came by and told us we had to abandon the house soon we knew we had to leave. The army wanted to give our house to their staff who was working to form the new provincial government in Battambang. They simply stated that we had to be out of the house in three days by 5:00 p.m. We told them "this was the house our father had built for the family" I told the soldiers that my family and I are going to be staying put. They asked us to prove that it was our house, knowing full well we could offer no proof since all records of ownership had been destroyed by the Khmer Rouge when they took over Battambang. We had no alternative but to leave so we decided to return to Wat Bote Wung where we had first lived after the Khmer Rouge had taken over.

In this village was a huge complex that had been built under the Khmer Rouge occupation where many of us from

Battambang ended up staying. We grabbed a little corner and set up a place for our family. Once again, our family was homeless, with nowhere else to go and no place to call home. We sat there, amongst the crush of people, trying to hide our sadness from those around us, who were, for the most part, experiencing the same feelings we were. What could we do? We had no power; we had no ability to prove anything about our ownership of the house. We had to resign ourselves to the fact that this is how life was and that we had better get used to it.

I knew that the family was going to need food, I walked to where my friend Jai lived and asked him what his food situation was and if he wanted to head out and look for food. He and his family were also starting to get hungry as they had just run out of food that they had managed to find so he agreed to head out with me. We decided to head out to the north of where we were and soon we came across a small farm where there were chickens wandering around. We snuck into the yard and tried to sneak up on the chickens but shortly realized there was no sneaking up on chickens. The chickens spotted us and started to run in circles around us as we tried to keep pace with them. We must have been crazy or really hungry because we kept up with them for as long as we could. I was hoping that we could wear the chickens out of energy. I saw a stick and whacked a couple of them and when Jai saw me swinging that stick he stopped his chase and started to laugh uncontrollably.

It did not take long for him to stop laughing. He was near some grass and saw a chicken head into the higher grass and as soon as he chased the chicken into the underbrush he stumbled upon a body that had been there for quite some time.

With his first step into the bush he slipped on the fat that had been leaching its way out of the body and then landed right on top of it and then the head fell off. We had never smelled anything so awful in our lives. This was a horrible reminder of how the Khmer Rouge felt about us. We were literally disposable to them. We gathered what we could carry from the farm and headed back to the village where the boiling pot was waiting for the chickens. We had boiled chicken and a green the Cambodians called Takuan. In Chinese, we call it Ong Choy which is also called water spinach. The stomachs of every one in the family were full and we managed to sleep well.

Several days later it was time for another run for food. We had a friend of mine named Nam who was living with us in our tent and I told him that it was his turn to come with me and find food for the family to eat. He and I left and walked for about one and a half hours and soon came upon a mango tree on an abandoned orange farm. We looked around, found a ladder, and scaled up the tree to start picking mangoes when all of a sudden I felt a cold sensation at the back of my neck and then just like that bullets started flying past us. We were so close to the front lines that we had accidentally stumbled into an active area.

We saw a couple of people who looked like they were running towards us who stopped, looked around and then when they figured out where the sound of the shooting was coming from, turned and ran away. But as soon as they were in the act of running again we saw them fall to the ground and we both realized that they had been shot dead. I turned from that grizzly sight and realized that there were still bullets whizzing through the leaves of the mango tree. I turned to my friend and yelled at him to get the hell out of there. I then took off running out to the dirt road calling out my friend's name. I looked around and realized that even though he had a limp he was ahead of me, running even faster than I was! I had never seen him move that fast ever. Once we were out of harms way, we stopped and had a laugh about how fast he had been running. Once Nam got his breath back he told me that he had never been that scared in his life and no matter how hungry he got he did not want to come that close to death for some damned mangoes! When the Khmer Rouge had been in power, I do not think I could have run away from anyone because I did not have the strength. But I was feeling better and getting stronger all the time because I was eating more regularly now.

Several weeks later, I was walking along the river heading south out of Battambang and headed into an empty village in search of food. I suddenly came across two Khmer Rouge soldiers who appeared to be quite young, maybe fourteen or fifteen years old. They came around the back of this little hut, one on each side of the hut, carrying AK-47s. They drew up their weapons and leveled them at me. I had a flashback to when I had been caught by the Khmer Rouge and I had not endured this much suffering only to die now. I drew out my machete and swung at the one on my left and hit him in the neck. I then drew out my axe and swung around and hit the other one on his shoulder. Blood started pouring from both their necks, and they dropped to the ground. I ran out of there as fast as I could. This was not an act of revenge but a gut reaction. I did not want to get killed by these two soldiers and I did what I had to do to stay alive another day. I knew that I had to get out of that are as quickly as possible.

Palm branches.

If anyone linked me with what had just happened other Khmer Rouge soldiers around the area would have hunted me down and killed me. I had heard many stories of how the Khmer Rouge killed people who stood up to them. They usually pulled your neck back and sawed into your throat with a palm leaf.

As I fled the village, I saw a small pig. Even in my panic I grabbed the little pig by its front leg. All of a sudden out of nowhere, someone else grabbed the pig too. So there were two of us pulling the pig in different directions. I knew that if I let go of it, there would be no food for my family that day. So I reached around and took out my machete and chopped that pig right in half. The blood spurted all over me. I grabbed the front part of the pig and put it in my sack and carried the pig home.

I gave the pig to my mom, who cooked it up that night. I couldn't eat any of it though. I was really shaken up from having to hack it like that and never wanted to kill another animal again. Once I had a chance to sit and relax, I mulled over the events of the day. I had most likely killed two men and chopped a pig in half to get food for my family. I couldn't stop thinking about those soldiers and what had happened to them. I struggled with the idea that I may have taken someone's life. Being raised by a Buddhist mother, we were taught never to take a man's life. Would my actions damage my karma? I didn't know what to think. All I knew for sure was that I was alive for another day and maybe that was enough.

Times were indeed dangerous and volatile. You never knew who was going to try to take advantage of you. Everyone was doing whatever they needed to survive. We still had to watch out for pockets of Khmer Rouge wherever we traveled but we also had to look out for fellow Cambodians. It was still hard to trust people. But then, surprisingly, help could come in unexpected ways.

One time, we were running low on grain, and my cousin said that they had some rice stored at a friend's house 32 kilometers away. They asked me to help get the rice because I still had a cow and a cart. We made the journey to fetch the rice, and on the way back, we came across some Cambodians standing around near the Oh Ta Ke Bridge. The group yelled at me saying "that cow is mine! It looks exactly like a cow I had. You are a thief and I want my cow back now". I thought for sure that a fight was going to take place over my cow. While we were yelling at each other some Vietnamese soldiers overheard what was happening and came over to see what all the yelling was about. They were stunned when I spoke to them in Vietnamese and I told them the people across the way were claiming that my cow was theirs.

The guards told me not to worry about it that they would take care of the problem. One of the Vietnamese soldiers who spoke a little Cambodian turned and yelled at the Cambodians to leave me alone. We managed to bring all the grain home safely.

My mother took whatever we found, put some aside some for our family and took the rest into town to trade for other goods at the market. One day she came across our Muslim friends who we lived with at the beginning of the Khmer Rouge occupation. Their family still lived by the Stunt Sangker River and told my mother that when they had extra fish they would bring us what they could spare. This action of kindess really touched my mother's heart so deeply. She told me that since my father had died she closed her heart off. I noticed a change in my mother after that. She opened up more, like her spirit had been nourished by the contact with her friends. Being shown even a simple act of kindness allowed her to open her eyes and see that not everything and everyone was bad.

While at the market several days later my mother ran into another lady who used to work for us. They talked for a while and her friend told her that she had extra rice and she would send her sons over with 23 kilograms (50 lbs)of rice. My mother cried at her generosity, saying "It is I who should be helping you out." Several days later her sons showed up, gave us the rice and in parting told us to always consider our two families as one.

We thanked them for their kindess and generosity. Giving someone 23 kilograms of rice was an amazing gift! Post Khmer Rouge gold and rice were the defacto currency of the country.

We could use part of the rice in trade for meat or some other need and still have enough to eat for a while.

Jackfruit

I remember one trip in particular that my brothers and I made to find food. We were about one hour away from where we lived and we came across a huge jackfruit tree. Near the tree was a huge ant hill full of red ants. The red ants were traveling up and down the tree and moving out to the leaves. They had ant hives all over the tree. Up in the tree, we could see some really good-looking huge jackfruits. First my brother tried to get up there, then our friend with the ox cart tried, then another brother tried to get up there, but none of them could handle the ants on the tree. Finally, I said, "Well, I will go up there and get that fruit. I am hungry and the jackfruit will make some nice meals for all of us."

I wrapped my pants tightly on my ankles and took my shirt off and tied it around the top of my pants. I started my way up with my one axe. I scaled the tree up to where the fruit was, and I hit that branch with all my might. Suddenly the ants were all over my head and torso. My whole head was red with the ants. Oh what painful bites they were. There seemed to be thousands of them sinking their little fangs into whatever skin they could find. But I kept on chopping that branch and finally it fell down.

Once I got down from the tree, everyone helped me clean the ants off of my body. I had them in my ears, on my eyelids, in my hair, in my pants, everywhere. I had so many bites on me that I was shaking from the pain. But we came home with nine jackfruit that day. I could not believe how good they tasted. I wondered if they tasted better because we had to work so hard to get the things. The only thing I know is that it was worth it.

Foraging for food often involved careful strategizing. On one trip we saw a cow wandering in a field. The cow seemed to belong to no one. We didn't dare take it ourselves, but a few minutes later, we came across a Vietnamese detail coming towards us on the path and we told them in Vietnamese about the cow. The Vietnamese would not just shoot and slaughter the cow for themselves, so instead, they shot the cow for us and we gave them the leg of cow as a token of our appreciation.

Later that same evening, we were crossing the dam back into town and came across another Vietnamese Army detail. We told them about all the fish above the dam. One of the Vietnamese shot a B-40 into the water and all the fish came floating up from the explosion. I found some rope, jumped into the water, and started gathering fish up for the Vietnamese and my brothers. We had just purchased salt so it made good sense to us to salt the fish right there on the spot. Everyone was happy because it had been many years since we had fish. We hadn't realized how much we missed eating fish. The meat was so tender and moist it was like eating a piece of heaven. Even today, I can still recall the taste of that fish.

Over the years of the Khmer Rouge occupation, many Cambodians became incredibly resourceful and became experts at making use of anything, whether it was edible or not. I vividly recall coming upon an empty tobacco field and saw an opportunity. We picked the tobacco, sliced it up, dried it and used it to trade for rice, meat or hard goods. It had been such a long time since I had had something to smoke. It felt really good to sit back and smoke. I never knew that a cigarette could taste so fine. I savored moments like this for all they were worth.

In addition to avoiding mines, unexploded ordinance, Vietnamese military, and the last Khmer Rouge stragglers we had to be careful not to get robbed on the way home. Making it home with food was actually quite dangerous. We were cautious about who we talked to and who we told when we left town in search of food. We had to hide whatever we found under grass and leaves in the ox cart. And we always returned to the city the back way. Everyone was starving, and thieving was rampant. People were even getting killed because they had fish or pork. The Khmer Rouge had destroyed so much of our culture that people had become vicious predators. This was especially shocking because pre-Khmer Rouge Cambodia had been a peaceful Buddhist country where people had generally felt safe everywhere. Peace had been an integral part of the culture. After having a common enemy in the Khmer Rouge, it was strange to have to protect ourselves from our fellow Cambodians, but this is what it had come to. Having made it this far, we were more determined than ever to survive.

MOVING ON

Our lives soon came to be dominated by the quest for food and other basic goods like clothing and shampoo. During the Khmer Rouge we never had any soap or shampoo or toothpaste and that made these items worth just as much as gold. The items were also hard to find because so many of us wanted to be able to feel clean again. People foraged and traded for absolutely everything. And of course, everyone was looking for food too, which made our task that much more difficult.

The longer we stayed where we were, the farther out we had to go to find anything substantial. The roots and plants that we used to gather by the river became harder and harder to find. There was no formal food distribution system within the country. There was no commerce. There was no infrastructure— no running water, no sewers—so cholera and typhus became rampant in the cities. There was no real government, and what little there was leaned toward the Communist ideology of the Khmer Rouge. Fighting was erupting everywhere as the Cambodian army and the Vietnamese army tried to defeat the Khmer Rouge, who were hiding in the jungle in western Cambodia. It was increasingly clear to us that it would be a long time before Cambodia returned to any kind of normalcy.

Then in late April, 1979, a few months after the Khmer Rouge fell, we began to hear rumors that large numbers of people were heading west to Thailand. The civil war was getting worse, and we couldn't stand this kind of fragile and unpredictable existence anymore. So our family decided to follow the crowds to Thailand. We felt we had no choice. We could stay in Cambodia and risk starving to death, getting shot, or getting blown up. Or, we could try to make it to Thailand, where there was at least hope that we could be safe from war and try to move forward with our lives.

I wanted to get an idea what exactly we were in for, so I decided to make the trip as far as the border with my cousin and his family before making the journey with my whole family. I left my family in Wat Bote Wung and headed out to the main road. Once I reached the road, I was stunned by what I saw: a river of people as far as the eye could see. There must have been thousands and thousands of people, all heading to Thailand. It was amazing to see that many people walking, pushing ox carts, riding bicycles in one direction, moving in unison in a slow, even pace towards the setting sun. We joined the sea of humanity, and I pushed the ox cart for my cousin for what seemed like an eternity. My legs strained and my back ached as I pushed and pushed until we stopped for the night. As I lay there on the ground trying to sleep I knew that I was going to have to somehow endure pushing the cart for the two day walk into Thailand.

My cousin had a gold leaf, with which he planned to bribe a Thai or Cambodian border guard. We knew the price to bring someone across the border was one ounce for eight people, and my cousin gave me 1/5 of an ounce of gold leaf. We spent the night in Gob, a village near the border, to prepare his family for the journey across. The next day, they crossed safely into Thailand. It was time for me to return and get my family. I was lucky because I was able to get a ride on a tractor all the way back to Wat Bote Wung. They were relieved to see that I had made it back safely. I told them that I had some gold that would help us pay our way into Thailand and that I knew how to get from our village to the crossing. We packed up what little we had and started out on the road towards Thailand, together this time.

There were a total of 15 of us traveling together. Some of us were pushing older relatives in wheelchairs. Others were assisting people who had been injured. Others carried whatever they could on their backs. We moved along the road slowly, slithering forward like a huge python, crawling its way along, trying to stay cool. We walked all day with the sun beating down on us. Along the way, the Cambodian Army tried to rob us. They held us for awhile as the army people searched the older ones in our group, looking for anything of value. No matter which way we turned, someone was trying to take what little we had. Then some Vietnamese soldiers showed up. My mother told them in Vietnamese what the Cambodian Army was up to. The Cambodians didn't want to cross the Vietnamese so they released us and we moved on as quickly as possible.

We spent the night by the roadside because we thought it would be safer than venturing too far into unfamiliar territory. Thankfully, we were all able to get some sleep because the next morning we wanted to make the crossing into Thailand.

We reached the border town in the late afternoon full of anticipation and still hoping to cross that day. But we got to the border too late, so we were forced to spend yet another night by the side of the road. There were more people than I had ever seen in one place in my life, all of them looking like weary broken-down travelers, most with nothing more than what was on their backs. You could hear tired children crying, people arguing with one another because someone had dared impinge on whatever little patch of dirt they called their own. The tension in the air was at a boiling point. Some of the people in this mass of humanity had walked from as far as Phonm Penh or Prey Veng, which were as far as 321 kilometers away. We were thirsty, hot, unbathed, hungry, and unsure of what lay ahead.

Cambodian citizens were in a state of limbo, unsure where we belonged anymore. The Cambodian government was still forming and really did not care if we left. The Vietnamese did not care if we left, and the Thai did not want us in their country at all. Thailand did not have the resources to deal with such an influx of people all pouring over the border at once. I do not know whether it was technically against Thai law for us to cross the border, but our backs were against the wall. We either had to cross or go back. Legality was irrelevant at this point. We just wanted out.

Early the next morning, local villagers started to lead people around us into the woods towards Thailand. I watched them closely as they led refugees away in exchange for a certain amount of gold per person. But I realized it was a scam. Once the refugees were already deep in the woods, the leaders just left them there and went off to gather more people—and their money. They never really took you all the way to Thailand. Abandoned in the woods, the refugees in the woods were then robbed. If they were lucky enough to make it back out of the woods alive, they found themselves still in Cambodia, right where they started, but with no more gold.

While some were getting led into the woods by Cambodian scammers, other refugees were being preyed upon by Thai thieves, who crossed into Cambodia to steal their gold. The thieves would show up with guns and knives and look for the weakest or the most sickly and beat them until the refugees gave them what ever they had. The thieves were like human vultures swooping in to pick what was left off the carcass. People tried to hide from the thieves in their makeshift shelters, beating them back with canes or sticks or rocks in a futile effort to protect what little they had left. We had all seen a lot in recent years, but the cruelty of these thieves still shocked us.

As a family, we decided the time had come to try to make the crossing. We gathered everyone up and headed into the woods. I was still holding the gold that I had gotten from my cousin. I knew that I needed to find a place on my person where the Thai guards would not think to look when they searched me. I decided to hide it in one of the patches in what I called my patch pants. These were the pants I had been wearing during the entire Khmer Rouge regime. I called them my patch pants because they had worn through and I had just kept on repairing them until they were mostly patches. I hoped the Thai would not think to look there.

Our family headed off into the woods blindly following the human trail into Thailand. There must have been hundreds if not thousands of us all desperately trying to cross the border. In our minds Thailand was like a shining light and the light was a chance at a better tomorrow, a brighter future than what lay behind us. Cambodia, no matter how close we held it to our hearts, was no longer the Cambodia we knew and loved.

When we got into the woods we soon realized that getting into the country was not going to be an easy task. We came across several Thai individuals whose only intent was to rob us. The thieves came up to us armed with knives and machetes and some were even carrying small handguns. All of us in that long line were ripe for the picking. We were trying to escape violence and many in that line were unarmed and had to let the Thai do whatever they wanted.

You see, families had taken their gold, melted it down and hid it inside of the women in the families. This was yet another humiliation to us. Our women were getting searched for gold and they were being very rough and treating the women badly. We had to just sit by and watch whatever degrading acts the Thai did to others and to us. The Thai were looking for rings, precious stones, gold, and silver, literally anything they could go and sell or trade. Our family, in a sense, was fortunate because by this time we really had nothing at all of value. We only had the clothes on our backs. The only thing of value was that little chunk of gold (maybe 1/5 of an ounce) that I managed to hide in my pants.

Once we made it to the Thai side of the border, we saw that all the refugees were confined to a 2-acre area that bordered the woods we had just left. The Thai army was patrolling the area keeping us penned inside the 2 acres. It's hard to say exactly, but I'm guessing there were some 50 thousand people crammed into this little patch of earth. As soon as we entered, the skies opened up and the monsoon rains started to fall in torrents, drenching us all. I looked around and saw that there was nowhere to hide. I knew that we had to get out of the rains quickly in case of lightning, which often accompanied the monsoons.

All we had to protect us was a small piece of plastic. I set up the plastic in the form of a lean-to and had my mother and the kids take refuge under it. Everyone else stayed out in the rain, hoping not to get sick. Before night fell, some of us went out into the jungle and dragged back a big log. We managed to start a fire to keep ourselves warm through the long wet night. That night was long and hard. I'd given up my jacket at the border, so I shivered my way through the night, waiting for the warmth of the day to take the chill out of my bones. Sitting there in that deluge, the rain beating down on my head, running down my face like a river run wild, I tried to imagine a better tomorrow, a place where I had a job and where I was warm and clean and dressed in new clothes and had a future.

The next morning did not get off to a good start. A group of Thai thugs arrived to steal our gold. I acted fast and sold our gold. Right after selling it, the first thing that I saw was a Pepsi. I was so overjoyed with the sight of that bottle! I had not tasted Pepsi in four years. I bought the liter bottle of Pepsi and drank it all in one gulp. Man that was the best tasting drink I have ever had in my life! I also bought a box of Top Ramen noodles and a dozen hard-boiled eggs. I ate the whole dozen eggs in one sitting. I had not had eggs in years, and once I started, I couldn't stop eating them. I also managed to stock up on some other food for my family.

I continued exploring the area across the Thai border and found someone cooking noodle soup. I told him that I grew up in a restaurant and that I was looking for a job. He agreed to take me on, along with my brother. The noodle stand would at least give us something to do and let us earn a little extra money. We got new clothes as part of the deal, and this was a great luxury. We were among the few refugees to actually have clothes that did not stink to high heaven. With what I earned daily, I could buy the family five Top Ramen and a can of sardines a day. Taking all things into consideration we were eating pretty well.

We had to be careful again of the Thai soldiers because they would just beat you on sight if you made them angry in any way. No matter which way we turned, there was no mercy. I think many of the Thai were under the mistaken impression that we had other options. But believe me, we would much rather have been back in our home city of Battambang, trying to get my father's house back and getting the restaurant running again. That would have been far preferable to sitting in this place that was neither here nor there; waiting for God knows what to happen to us.

Even though people did not have a lot of money, our little noodle stand was extremely busy. People were so hungry that they would sit down and eat two or three bowls just because they could! For years, Cambodians had been so starved by the Khmer Rouge that whenever there was food now, we ate as much as our stomachs could hold. People would sit and drink coffee for hours on end because they had some time to relax. Even though we had no idea about what was going to happen to us, we enjoyed getting together with friends over a cup of coffee in the morning, which is a big tradition in Cambodia. In fact, to this day, I still take time to enjoy coffee with friends whenever I can.

TO THAILAND AND
BACK AGAIN

We remained stuck just inside of Thailand for several frustrating weeks until one day; all of a sudden the Thai army announced that buses would soon be showing up. They explained that the United Nations had set up a camp for us to go to and that there was an island for all of us. Although we weren't totally clear on what was in store for us, we were eager to move on from where we were. And sure enough, the buses soon pulled up. Once I saw the buses I ran over to where my employers noodle stand was and I talked with him about what was going on. He told me to grab as much food and clothing as I could carry so I immediately put as much food as I could into some boxes so I could carry them on the bus with me.

When I got back to where the buses were I heard the soldiers yelling "Ok, all the Cham get on this bus" and "Cambodians, come over here" and "Chinese here." It was pandemonium for a while, but eventually all of us were separated in to our own little groups. As I was getting on the bus, I asked a guard what was going on. He went on to tell me one of the biggest lies I had ever heard. According to him, the U.N. had rented an island for all the refugees and the buses were all taking us to the boat that would take us to the island. What had all of us believing them was that they gave us a bag of food with a boiled egg and some bread and an orange or two. So we were all thinking "maybe this is true and we are going to a better camp!"

We finally left the area in the early afternoon and drove for several hours. I tried to track where we were going by watching the sun, but I could only glimpse it every once in a while. If I looked out too often, the guard on the bus would order me to pull my face from the window. I think we were on the buses for about 14 hours or so. Finally the buses stopped and the lights went out. I told my mother that something was wrong. It was dark, and I suddenly saw a lot of flashlights. The people holding the lights were dressed in army clothes and the soldiers were wearing the ga ma (neckerchief), and they were all holding machine guns and rifles. I panicked, as a thought popped into my brain: "Oh man, they sent us back to be killed by the Khmer Rouge."

I surveyed the scene, trying to get as much information as I could. I saw people sitting by the side of the road with their bags. We were on top of Preahvihear Mountain, far from anything. It turns out we were actually right next to Cambodia—one side, on top of the mountain was Thailand and the other side was Cambodia. They had gotten all of us off the buses and we were sitting outside, waiting for who knows what. Then, as soon as the sun rose, we all heard a machine gun start firing and soldiers yelling, "GO! GO! GO! Run down the mountain!" After coming all this way, the Thai were actually forcing us right back into Cambodia! I found my boxes of food on the bus, gathered up my family and hurriedly put food in their pockets, in their knapsacks and *gama's* and then we were told to line up.

With machine guns at our backs, we had no choice but to run. But as we started down the mountainside, we heard explosions. I realized the mountain side was mined and that we could all get blown up. What on earth were the Thai doing to us? We wanted to run down the mountain as fast as possible but I had to tell my family to walk as fast as they could and to follow the person in front of them exactly. We needed to stay on the trail in order to avoid the mines. The whole mountain side was in a state of utter chaos.

As I neared the bottom of the mountains, I started seeing bodies that had been blown up. Out of the corner of my eye, I saw a stack of bodies and dismembered limbs. There were some people who had stepped on mines but had not been killed. They were lying by the side of the trail moaning in pain and crying out for someone, anyone to help them. We could do nothing for those who were still alive because we could not take the chance of getting blown to bits ourselves. We did not know where the mines were and to stop and move towards them even a little bit could have killed us. I told our family members that we need to stay together all the way down the hill. I looked to my left, and, in a nearby tree, I saw a mine sitting in the branches. At the bottom of the hill, we all had to stop because there was no where else to go. We were deep in the woods and there were many people who were starting to huddle together, all afraid for their lives. We tried to get information from anyone we could but no one knew anything. Every once in awhile someone would lose it and turn and run up the mountainside. As soon as they got near the top of the mountain the Thai army would open fire on the runner and force them back down the mountain. It seemed the Thai had solved their refugee problem.

We were effectively trapped and would have to figure out our options, but for the time being, we had more immediate concerns. It had been hours since we had anything to drink, so my brother and I went to look for water. At the bottom of the hill, there was a stream. But since it was the dry season, there was little water in it. We started to follow a trail that people before us had beaten down. Along the way, we came across someone who had stepped on a mine and was still alive. He lay face down, and he was in terrible shape: his face was charred, and some of his insides were hanging out. He was moaning loudly and convulsing. We could do nothing for him, as we were all afraid that he might be lying on another mine. Watching a fellow human being die made us feel helpless and incredibly sad and compounded all the other emotions we were feeling right then. I kept on asking myself, "Is this what it has come to? Our lives broken down to the point where this is all there is? Is there anyone in the world who cares what is happening to us?" A true feeling of despair descended on me at that point. Although I can't speak for the others around me, I could see from the looks in their eyes that we were all experiencing the same emotional trauma.

There was nothing for us to do but carry on. We slowly headed past this man and followed the trail to the creek. When I got down there, I saw a body lying face down in the water. It looked like he had been blown up near the creek side and landed in the creek. People all around us were yelling and cursing, shoving people out of their way to reach the water. No one seemed to care that there was a dead body lying there and that the water was most likely contaminated.

We were all stuck there on the side of that hill for two weeks, drinking the water with the body floating in it the whole time. I do not know if anyone got sick or died, but the body had been there long enough for it to break down, and the fat had dissolved into the water. To get to the water, we had to use our hands to part the layer of human fat that floated on top of the water. Afterward, our hands were covered with this bad smelling grease. It was a terrible sight and an even worse smell. I went further down the trail to look for clean water and came across many bodies. Once I came across a family with three small children and the mother and father had been killed and the children were sitting next to the bodies of their parents, crying at the top of their lungs. That was very hard to see, and I've never been able to erase that image from my mind.

All this time, I was becoming very afraid that my mother was not going to make it. She was getting very skinny. She had once been a fairly heavy-set woman, and I think she lost about eight clothes sizes. Ever the faithful Buddhist, my mother prayed to my father every day to come help us out of the mess we found ourselves in. She told me that she had a dream that her husband had come up behind her, hugged her and told her that we were going to be ok.

One small blessing was that we still had food from my employer to tide us over. This was a big help because we could not really move anywhere unless someone else moved around us, so it was nearly impossible to go foraging. We were very careful to measure out the food since we did not know how long we were going to be stuck on this mountain.

All the family had was a tarp to sit on, and if we needed to go to the bathroom, we dug a hole with a stick and just went right there. We then covered up the hole and moved the plastic over it. People covered every square inch and did all their living right out in public: sleeping, getting water, living, and dying. But I think the hardest part was trying not to go insane from the crush of an unwashed, filthy, stinking humanity all around us and the onslaught of humidity, which was so thick it hurt to breathe. Just consider the reality of fifty thousand people needing to relieve themselves every day. And then there were the dead bodies, which were everywhere. Sometimes you could not walk a foot or two without slipping on a decomposing body. I can still recall the stench of that hillside even in my worst dreams.

In addition to all this when we went to get water, we had to be very careful to stay on the trails because no one knew where the mines were. For all we knew, one step in any direction we would be blown to hell. One morning, we were walking in line to get some water, and a fellow passed us off the trail. We all yelled at him, "Stop! Get on the trail! Get on the trail!" But it was too late. All of a sudden, we heard a noise, saw a puff of smoke, and he was gone, just like that. We could find nothing left of him.

Between the mines and the crowding and the quest for water, that hillside was one of the most dehumanizing places I have ever set foot. To this day, I cannot fathom how or why the Thai would do this to us. All we wanted was to get out of the mess that Cambodia had become. We had left Cambodia in hopes of finding a better life. To end up here, on this fetid, rotting slope of humanity was a cruel twist of fate that no one in my family could make sense of.

While all of this was going on my oldest brother (Tong Meng) got very sick, so sick he could no longer walk. We found some bamboo and a couple of old rice sacks and fashioned a hammock of sorts between the bamboo sticks and made a stretcher so we could carry him with us. I realized that we had to somehow move off that hillside if we were going to survive. So we slowly, painstakingly, started to walk out, figuring that any place we arrived would have to be better than this. But the crush of humanity around us was staggering. It took at least an hour to walk the equivalent of a city block. We weren't sure which way to go, so we followed the stream away from the hill and towards what looked like a main road. Eventually the stream got deeper and there was more water, so we made our little camp there. It wasn't much, but we had at least managed to leave the madness of that hillside behind us.

We stayed near the stream for a couple of nights to gather our strength and to drink a little clean water. On the day we were trying to leave our little camp, we heard an explosion up the way. We found out that the Vietnamese army was in the area trying to help the rest of the people off the hill. The soldiers were telling people to head down this road. They were saying to go west if you wanted to head to Thailand and east for Kompong Thom. Unfortunately, while helping the refugees, one of the soldiers stepped on a mine and blew himself up. We were thankful to the Vietnamese for helping people move on.

The Khmer Rouge looked upon them as the enemy and tried to force us into being afraid of them, but the Vietnamese seemed to be the only ones looking out for us.

We finally made it to the main road. Full of despair and extremely worried at our family member's failing health, we made the decision to follow the crowds and headed back to Battambang. We walked at least 32 kilometers a day for a month. Many days, it rained. We took turns carrying my brother and we were all pushed to the extreme edge of exhaustion. My shoulders swelled up and my feet were so painful that each step brought excruciating pain. I did not think I would be able to walk another step, but I somehow kept going. We had to get my brother home.

During our journey, we came across some Vietnamese soldiers. My mother began to speak with them in Vietnamese, asking them if we could leave our brother with them. They agreed to take care of him. This was heartbreaking for all of us, but if we did not find a safe place to leave him, he was going to die. And if we continued carrying him, we were going to die. We spent the night near the soldiers, and the next morning, we told him that we loved him and that we thought his chances of staying alive were better with the soldiers than with us. After an emotional goodbye, we left my brother, his wife, and their daughter and continued on towards Battambang. After we left our brother my mother started to shake uncontrollably. We had seen these symptoms before and thought she might have contracted malaria. She never complained, she never said she was sick; she just kept on walking in step with us.

We walked steadily, slowly towards our destination. We stopped only when we had to, mostly to eat and or drink water or rest by the side of the road at night. There were Vietnamese stationed every 40 kilometers or so, who gave us flour or salt and rice. We added water to the flour to make a thick paste, then stuck a branch through the paste and roasted it over the fire. One day we were told by fellow travelers to be careful because the Khmer Rouge was still active in the area. If they caught you, they would slit your throat. So we walked in the forest and stayed off the main roads.

Occasionally, we found cigarette butts. We dried them out, removed the tobacco, and rerolled them to smoke. This helped alleviate our hunger pains a bit. People were reluctant to help travelers passing through. One night we asked a woman if we could stay on her property under her tree, but she said no because the last people who had stayed had tried to steal her things.

I was still very concerned about my mother because she was getting very tired and losing even more weight. Whenever we stopped, we had to make sure that we could find wood, so that we could create a lean-to. This way, she could stay out of the weather a little bit and stay dry at night. The rest of us slept out in the elements, often getting soaked to the bone and shivering all night long. We slept with our food clutched in our arms all night so that no one would steal it from us. That was our biggest concern, making it through the night without someone stealing our food or killing us for it. I sharpened up my axes with religious regularity in case I had to defend the family.

Soon we passed through the Iron Hill area. My family and I were resting by the side of the road and I saw the lady that I had wanted to marry back in 1976. She was in a group of people walking in the same direction as we were. I was very surprised and extremely happy to see her and it made my heart feel warm with tenderness. It had been too long since I had felt anything like that. She saw me and smiled and said a very soft "Hello" to me. I smiled back warmly and watched her walk slowly away and thought "this may be the last time I ever see her." Even though I was with my family a sudden feeling of emptiness permeated my soul. I turned, looked at them and said "we need to get on our way." We gathered together what little we had, stood up to shake out the pain and continued on. Mindlessly, we fell in with the rest of the people heading down the road, heads down, marching towards an unknown future. As we were walking we talked amongst ourselves and made the decision to stop and rest in Kompong Thom. I knew from looking into my mother's eyes that she really needed a break. We stayed several nights in the area on the side of the road near a Vietnamese Army contingent. My mother decided to strike up a conversation with a Vietnamese soldier at one of the food stands and was told "there is a truck coming through the next day that will be able to take us to Sisophon" which is only 64 kilometers from Battambang. It would only take a couple of days for us to walk the distance and get home. It seemed that we were finally reaching the end of our journey.

BACK IN BATTAMBANG

he next day, the truck arrived and took us to Sisophon. The truck driver delivered us to an area just outside of Sisophon, helped us off the truck and told us to wait there and someone would be by to help us. There were many people there just like us. Displaced and nowhere to go and waiting for whatever was next in life. When they dropped us off, it was late afternoon, almost dusk. Soon after, what appeared to be officials showed up carrying clipboards.

They identified themselves as organizers for the new Cambodian government, and their job was to assist people in getting back to their home villages and cities. When the organizers got to our family, they asked us our names and how many family members were in our group and where we were from. We felt compelled to tell them because of their official status, but this made us very nervous. We were afraid the authorities would punish us for trying to abandon the country and send us off to some kind of jail or camp. We had a quick family meeting and decided to leave the area right away. The very next morning, we started on the road to Battambang.

On the road out of Sisophon, I came across a Cambodian fellow who I knew from the old days. He knew I was a cook and asked me if I knew how to make Pat lo, which is a very popular dish consisting of meat (typically chicken or pork) and a special herb-soy sauce. Although there was no soy sauce in Cambodia (another side effect of the Khmer Rouge—they destroyed the manufacturing plants that made soy sauce), I said that I could. The fellow told me if I wanted to cook for him, he would split a third of the profits with me as well as feed me twice a day. I had no money and no job prospects, so I decided to stay in Sisophon and take the fellow up on his offer. I told my family of the job offer and sent them on their way back to Battambang. Part of my plan was to take most of the money I made and send the cash home to my family. Before I started this job I needed to clean myself up because I was really dirty and smelled even worse.

I needed a bath and a haircut before I could start cooking, so my new boss helped me get cleaned up. Getting to stand under hot water and take a shower brought tears to my eyes. I was overjoyed to feel the spray of hot water on my face and body again. I tried as hard as I could to breathe in the water like it was the perfume on a woman's neck. To actually be clean and smell good again was like putting on new skin. I really felt reborn, as if my eyes were opening again. I hardly recognized my new self and was surprised at how much a thorough cleaning could change my perspective.

After the shower, I started to gather what I needed to make the sauce. In the absence of official soy sauce, I had to improvise. I got a big pot and crumbled up brown sugar into it with some water, salt and MSG and started to boil it down. I made hoisin sauce with mung beans, which I boiled down and mashed up. I added some tamarind and chilies and mixed everything together. It came out tasting like a sweet and sour sauce with a spicy kick. Quite good I might add. After a few more batches of the sauce I had it perfected so I knew it was time to start cooking. I cut my meat and marinated it to perfection and threw it into boil. Soon the heavenly smell of the cooking meats filled the street. It did not take long for word to get around that there was this fellow down the street who was making great Pat Lo and soon I had a loyal clientele who stopped by to watch me go through the process of making it. I knew the fellow I was working for was making a lot of money off of this food that I was cooking and I had not seen any money in my pocket yet.

It came time for me to get paid, but my business partner did not mention anything about paying me, so I decided to confront him. When I finally worked up the nerve to ask him for the money he owed me, he told me in no uncertain terms "I am not going to pay you". He went on to say "I am not making any money and you are staying in my house eating two meals a day." I stared at him in disbelief when he talked to me like that. Even more, I was amazed he thought eating and sleeping could be considered compensation. What was even worse was I was not staying inside of his house. I was sleeping on the cart every night, getting rained on and shivering through the night. I was in a rage. I still had a lot of pent-up anger at the world, and my first thought was that I wanted to kill this guy and burn down his house. I took a long slow breath in to control myself and on the exhale I started to talk to him. I was very honest and told him I knew he was making a lot of money because I saw how much food was being sold. I was counting the number of people who came and bought food and I saw the amount of gold that came across the cart. I continued by telling him, "Our cart is the most popular because my recipe is the best in town and without my recipe you would not make money." I tried hard to keep the recipe a secret, even from my partner. Even customers tried to trick me into giving away my secrets by saying things like, "Hmmm, it tastes like you use this spice or that spice in there… most unusual. Tell me, please, what is that flavor?" Despite my best efforts, the fellow I was working for ended up with my recipe. I was furious, but continued working for him for a while because I had nowhere else to go. Since my boss was not going to pay me for cooking Pat lo I was going to have to go to work for myself somehow.

I had thought about borrowing some gold from my now ex-boss to start doing some trading so I worked up the nerve to ask my boss to lend me some gold. I wanted to return to the Thai border and do some trading. Cambodians from all walks of life were coming and going across the border to bring things back home because there was literally nothing in our country. People came back with food, clothes, shoes, whatever they could carry and sell. I decided it was a good way to make some money. He agreed to loan me seven tenths of an ounce of gold, which I would have to pay back at 30 percent. I headed to the closest border town with a Cambodian friend of mine, which was a two-day journey on foot. The trip was dangerous because there were Khmer Rouge stragglers in the area, unscrupulous border guards at the border, and groups of bandits looking to rob unsuspecting travelers. I was extremely determined to give it a try despite the risks.

On our first trip, we headed to a small village where we had heard people were getting across fairly easily. The village was near a forest that straddled the two countries. The locals charged a fee to show people the way across the Thai border. It was safest to travel in groups to avoid being targeted by robbers.

My friend and I spent the night in the woods next to the border. We awoke to the sound of people crossing the river next to us, so we got up and crossed the river behind them, following another group to avoid having to pay our way. It was a sketchy, hard-hearted place, and my friend and I were so afraid of what might happen we swore to each other we would be willing to kill and or die for each other. We were committed to doing this, so we just kept following the trail and hoped we'd be ok.

As we got close to the border, I told my friend to let me do the talking since I spoke some Thai. I took out my machete, checked it to make sure it was still sharp (very sharp indeed) and readied myself in case we came upon someone with bad intentions. We emerged from the woods on the Thai side in mid-afternoon. We arrived in a huge field full of people. There must have been close to a thousand people there doing as much business as they could before they were discovered by the Thai border patrol. If the Thai border patrol showed up, everyone ran in separate directions and tried to escape. We knew many had been killed attempting to do the very thing we were setting out to do, so we wanted to get our business done quickly.

The first thing we did was locate the gold dealer a friend of ours told us about. I told my friend to stand behind the second person (when doing deals like this, the Thai would travel in pairs as a safety precaution) and hold the machete out. If they made a move to rob us, he was to chop the person's head off and we would run. The Thai were also known to carry small handguns that could easily be carried in a pocket or in the palm of one's hand. Basically, no one trusted anyone, which made these transactions pretty risky.

We found our gold trader quickly, did the trade safely, bought what we wanted (staples like condensed milk, sugar, rice, and cigarettes, whatever we could sell easily), and left the same way we came in—as quickly as we could. We made it across the border without incident and immediately came upon a long line of Cambodians trying to leave. We crossed the huge line, and hopped into the woods. As soon as we hit the woods, we got hit by rain. We hunkered down for the night under a piece of plastic tarp my buddy had packed, leaned back to back, and slept as much as we could in between rain storms. As soon as the sun came up, we pulled ourselves together, worked the aches out of our bones, and left for home. We arrived back in Sisophon a day and a half later and sold our goods at the public market. I settled my debt with my employer. All in all, it was a successful trip: I made a small profit on the gold, learned how to get across the border safely, made it back alive and was able to send gold back to my mother and sister in Battambang. In fact, it was such a success we immediately started to plan the next one. And in between trips, I continued to make my Pat lo.

About one week later, we were off again. However, our second trip started out on a bad note. We had decided to try to get in to Thailand by another route because we had heard there were some skirmishes between Cambodian troops and the

Khmer Rouge on our original route and we definitely wanted to avoid getting messed up in that. We got across the border without any trouble, and as soon as we hit the woods we got lost almost immediately. We wandered around for about six hours. To make matters worse, we did not have any water with us. We wandered around in the elephant grass, lost, afraid, hungry, and disoriented by the tall grass towering over our heads.

We eventually got to a place where the grass was shorter. I popped my head out to get our bearings, only to see a Khmer Rouge army detail scouring the woods ahead of us. They saw me, and in my shock I just about fell on my butt. I managed to regain my composure enough to hear them ask me, "Hey, do you know where there is any water around here?" I calmly told them to head down the trail to a pool of water in the river. I turned to my friend, who saw me shaking with fear, and told him, "Let's get the hell out of here as fast as we can!"

And that's just what we did. We were so afraid we aborted our trip and high tailed it back home. When I saw the Khmer Rouge detail out there like that, I just assumed they were going to slit my throat. The Khmer Rouge had still not given up and was still actively fighting in parts of the country. There were rag-tag groups in and around the densely forested hillsides and jungle areas all around the Thai border.

Our third trip got off to a much more auspicious start. We made it to the border without incident, bought our goods and had some money left over for food for ourselves for the trip home. We were both carrying packs weighing about 80 pounds. We walked out of Thailand, crossed into Cambodia, and got lost in the woods again. This was the dry time of year when it is most hot and humid. As we carried these packs, we were losing water and getting very close to being completely dehydrated. We rested when we could and walked at night to avoid the heat of the day. We both heard this ringing in our ears and were getting dizzy. We knew if we did not find something to drink soon, we might die of thirst. After walking for what seemed like days, my buddy sat down and said, "Man, what the hell! When we were over there, I bought a liter of Pepsi. I was going to save it for my wife and kid, but if we don't drink this, we'll die out here." That Pepsi saved us. We decided to drink only a couple of sips whenever we really felt we needed it to make it last. I never knew a Pepsi, even warm, could taste that damn good!

This new business model was working out so well we decided to make another trip, but things got out of hand quickly this time. On our way out of Thailand, the Thai army showed up at the border area. There had been reports of a Khmer Rouge detail wandering around near the border and they had made the mistake of crossing over into Thailand. Suddenly, I was witnessing a stand off between the two forces. I saw one of the smaller Khmer Rouge pull up a B-40 (a bazooka). Both sides were armed and ready, staring each other down like in one of those old westerns I used to watch in the theaters.

My buddy and I looked at each other and without saying a word turned and ran deeper into Thailand to wait for the craziness to die down. I found the person I had sold the gold to and told him I wanted to buy the gold back. He was with three very tough-looking people, and they were all doing some gambling. When the lead guy handed me my gold, I told him it was not enough. The lead guy grabbed this necklace I was wearing, and two of the thugs stood up behind him with their arms crossed. I pulled out my axe and yelled, "Do you know who I am? I am not afraid of you!" I swung the axe and slashed him in the face. My friend was backing me up with his machete, and they realized we had no fear. They wanted nothing more to do with us. They gave us our gold back in a hurry, and we ran off. We made it back home without further incident.

Back in Sisophon, I was sitting out on the stoop when one of my brothers (Kheang) went riding by. When he saw me, he pedaled his bike back, jumped off, and came running over to me. It was such a surprise it took me a second or two to realize who it was. We talked for quite a while, and he told me our uncle was looking to open a noodle shop in Sisophon up on the hillside just out of town. This uncle had a broken arm and was not able to get the shop up and running. Would I like to help?

This was a great offer. I needed to find a better place to live than on this cart, and I looked forward to working with someone who would pay me and whom I could trust. This was a pretty good deal in those days. Even several months after the Khmer Rouge regime, most people still had nothing. We used to say Cambodia was like an empty house. Times were so tough if someone lay still long enough on the street, people would stop and take the clothes off the person lying there. No one had money, and it took a lot of bribes even to be able to open up the shop my uncle was planning. Things were rebuilding, but ever so slowly.

I decided I wanted to sell Pat lo at my uncle's café. I worked up the nerve to ask my uncle if I could borrow some gold. I told him I'd like to use the gold to buy meat for my recipe. My uncle gave me a long look in the eye, looked me up and down, looked at the ring on his finger, took the ring off and gave it to me. He did not say much except I was to repay him as soon as possible. The ring was one quarter of an ounce of gold, which was a princely sum to me. I took the ring to the butcher in the public market and handed him the ring. He asked me how much meat I wanted, and then he took a pair of wire cutters to the ring, cut off a small part of it, and dropped it into his little gold scale. He weighed out the meat and I was on my way. I made the sauce that I had perfected earlier and started to sell Pat lo again.

Within a week, I had more than enough gold to pay back my uncle. I sold a lot of the barbecue every day. We had a lot of volume at the café because of the barbecue and because my uncle's café was in a good spot in the market. There were cafés all around us that had already been established, but soon we were doing more business than any other cafe. I knew it was my secret recipe at work again. A strange fury arose in me when I thought back to how my former employer had ripped me off. I had always known he was making money hand over fist. He treated me badly at a time when I could have really used the money to help support my family. However, I knew I had to leave this to karma. I felt lucky that my situation was improving.

All of the gold I made I took it and sent it back to Battambang to help support my mother and sister. I also heard from a family friend that my oldest brother (Tong Meng) was in the hospital in Kompong Thom. I wanted to send some gold over to my brother to help him tend to his hospital needs, and a friend offered to bring the gold to him. I was skeptical. You never knew who to trust, even with old friends, because so much had changed during the Khmer Rouge years. I took a chance on him, and my friend made it all the way to Kampong Thom and delivered the gold (all without getting robbed along the way). I was glad I had not completely lost the ability to trust people and there were still good people out there willing to stay true to their word. When my friend returned he told me that the soldiers had been kind enough to drive him to the hospital when we left him. They took care of him all the way there and brought his wife and child with them. I was so worried about scams and mistaken identity (which were both rampant around this time) that I didn't quite let myself believe it. Plenty of unscrupulous people were in the business of latching on to a family's misery and taking their money in exchange for finding the missing. Family members were constantly being misled by their hope of reuniting with loved ones. It was because of all these things that I was hearing that I was concerned for my brother because he had no money. Money meant you could receive better care in the hospital and might even get a private round-the-clock nurse.

Meanwhile, I worked away at the cafe making my Pat lo barbecue. I earned gold to send home, and was living a little more comfortably than I had in a long time. I started to gain some weight back after the forced starvation and really enjoyed simple pleasures, like eating and smoking, again. One day while I was cooking one of Tong Meng's close friends came in to see me. He told me he was a truck driver whose regular route took him through Kompong Thom. I asked him to check on my brother and he agreed.

One month later, Tong Meng's best friend showed back up in Sisophon, and brought with him my brother, his wife and child! I was so happy to see them and to be together again. I had feared that I may never have the joy of being with my brother again. I walked up to him, grabbed each shoulder, looked him in the eye and then gave him a long embrace. I said to him, "You are so skinny. Let me feed you some good food!" I went and cooked up food for everyone. When he was done eating he asked me for a smoke and as soon as he finished smoking he passed out. I had to catch him before he hit the floor. My brother and his family stayed in the area for awhile, and we reminisced about old times as he worked on getting his strength back.

Before my brother had gotten out of the hospital, I had received a letter from his father-in-law in Thailand. He asked me to tell my brother to contact him whenever I saw him. The instructions were for me to go to the border area and make contact with a couple of vendors he knew. Those vendors would go to Thailand and contact the father-in-law, and he would come to the border to get them. The father-in-law had crossed into Thailand one month after the Khmer Rouge took over in Cambodia and he lived in a village called Aran. He had Thai citizenship, which we hoped would make it easier for our family to stay there. I made contact with the vendors on behalf of my brother and returned back home. I sent for my family in Battambang, thinking it would be a good idea for my brother to take my mother, sister, and her son out of the country with them and because I was working I had saved enough money to help them with travel expenses.

GETTING MARRIED

eanwhile, right around this time, I met my future wife. Kim was the niece of my uncle's partner, and she worked as a dishwasher at the café. I was always teasing her while we were in the kitchen.

It may sound surprising to a western audience, but arranged marriages have been the tradition in Cambodia for centuries. It made perfect sense to me to have my aunt work on arranging my marriage. I realized I was pretty much homeless and had very little to offer. If they were willing to accept me as a husband, I'd be grateful. I always appreciated this about Kim. Even though I had nothing at this point in my life, she was willing to take me as her husband. I always felt we were put together for a reason, for a special purpose in this life.

Traditionally, marriage was always arranged without the knowledge or consent of the individuals to be married. Forced marriage was common. Many families arranged marriages while the betrothed individuals were still very young; friends made promises to each other that their children would marry. If a man was interested in marrying a girl he saw but to whom he had not spoken, his parents would arrange an engagement ceremony with the girl's parents. The girl had no say in the matter. These days, marriage is still arranged but individuals often are consulted about the choice of their spouse, and rejecting the parents' arrangement is tolerated. Even a young woman has an opportunity to reject her parents' wishes, although not many daughters are yet willing to exercise this option. I was happy I was able to find someone who was willing to be with me and work alongside me to make our lives better. Having someone to share life and grow old together with is part of the beauty of life. I was fortunate to have met Kim.

The day before we were to be married, the market place where my uncle's café was located suddenly closed indefinitely. We were told the public market was built on government land and they wanted to build a government building on that spot. It meant that I was going to start out my married life without a job, with no income and no savings. Ever since I had started working at the café, I had sent all I earned to my mother to support the rest of the family. Suddenly, here I was, getting ready to start my own journey with a new wife, and I had nothing to my name.

Fortunately, my future mother-in-law gave me some gold so I could take care of pre-marriage ceremonies. She told me to go home and take care of the traditional worship of ancestors. I cooked several dishes of food. I went to the well, got some water, cleaned up and went to pray to the ancestors. That was a heartbreaking moment because I prayed to my dad to protect me and my new wife as we started out new lives together. I prayed to him, "You left in peace and are living in peace. Please keep your spirit around us to protect us." Later that day we performed our ceremony and got officially married in front of my mother-in-law and Kim's uncles. About 20 family members from both sides joined us to celebrate afterward, sharing the food I had prepared beforehand. After the festivities, we returned to my mother-in-law's place, where we had started staying since the café closed. Kim and I sat down with some tea and started to get to know each other better. She told me she was glad she married me because I was someone her younger brothers could look up to, and was someone who would always help out the family. She felt safe around me and knew I would protect her.

A couple of days after the wedding, I had to move my mother-in-law to a camp outside of town. It was kind of remote and far from any kind of foot traffic, so we couldn't open a business there. I knew the time was coming when I would soon have to make some big decisions about my family's future. One option, of course, was to stay and hope things would get better, though we had no idea how long it would take the country to get beyond the Khmer Rouge-inflicted hell we still found ourselves in. The other was to try to leave the country again and start all over elsewhere. Neither would be easy.

Around this time, I got wind of some news blowing out of Thailand. The rumor was that Thailand was going to allow an outside group to establish a refugee camp called Freedom Camp. I sat down with all the people under my care at that time (Kim, her mother and Kim's four younger brothers and three younger sisters), and I said to them, "It is time for us to try something else. Let's go to Thailand and try our luck there." I figured anywhere was going to be better than this precarious state of limbo we found ourselves in.

I felt it was time to go since most of my family was already in Freedom Camp. The only family members that I had in Cambodia at this time were my brother's Kheng in Battambang and Kok Kheang in Sisophon.

I heard from family that my sister-in-law also wanted to leave Cambodia. I went to Battambang where they were living and brought them back to Sisophon. There were four people in the group, his widow and three children. I gathered up Kim's family and had a meeting with them about what we should do. All at the meeting agreed we should make our way into Thailand. The next thing I had to figure out was the logistics: who would go, when, and how we would get there.

My brothers-in-law and I rode our bikes into Battambang, gathered up my brother's family, and got out of there as quickly as we could. We headed straight for the border. At this point, we were a sizeable group as there were 15 of us traveling together. We decided to head straight for the woods (which were safer than the roads), we came upon a dead soldier who was wearing the uniform for the new government. He had been shot in the head, and it looked like he had not been dead very long. This worried my brother-in-law because it meant there was Khmer Rouge lurking around in the woods. The last thing we wanted was to run into them. With so many people in our group, including several children, we could never have escaped.

We figured our best option was just to keep going and hope for the best. We walked around the body and continued walking slowly west towards the Thai border. After several hours, we crossed safely into Thailand and reached Freedom

Camp. The Freedom Camp had been set up for the endless stream of refugees leaving Cambodia. There must have been upward of a hundred thousand people there when we arrived. There were people as far as the eye could see; new arrivals were setting up their little areas for their families while those who had been there longer were just going about the business of getting through the day.

We walked around Freedom Camp until we found a spot to sit and stay. We staked out our area and dug a little moat around the outside of it so when it rains the water would hopefully stay in the moat. We went out in the woods and found some trees and broke some branches off to use to brace up our tarp to make a tent. The whole family stayed in the tent. I think we had two tents at the time for all the people we had with us. It was quite hard. We had no beds so we slept on the ground every night. It was a fight to sleep because of the bugs that crawled on the ground. We had to watch out for snakes and all sorts of things that crawled in the night. Centipedes were always a constant danger.

Every day the young men in the family left the camp in the never ending search for food and water. The more things got used up around the camp area the further we had to trek to find things to eat and to get decent water. As we learned very quickly, the camp was a hard place to live. We had to hustle every single day just to get by. There was no government or aid-organization support for this camp, so we were all on our own. You had to find your own food, dig your own toilet, and find grass and wood to make huts. We were all fighting for limited space and resources. Tensions ran high, and we all learned to watch our backs at all times. I realized I needed to do something fast to start making some money and trading seemed to be my best bet. I started trading and selling on the Cambodian side of the border. The money I made enabled us to eat and stock up on a few staples and since the trips had been made without any problems I felt pretty secure I could bring family members with me.

On my next trip I decided to take my little brother Chai. It was extremely hot that day, I did not wear a shirt, only jeans. I had learned to leave a little money in one pocket and hide the rest somewhere else on my body. I left 50 baht in my left back corner pocket and tied 3000 baht to my right ankle with a rubber band. We bought our Thai goods and started to cross the border with a big group of traders, but we ran across a Thai border patrol. They opened fire on us with machine guns and grenade launchers. It didn't take long for them to round us all up. I think there were about 30 of us, including some Cambodian Freedom Fighters. For some reason I do not know the Thai army really despised the Freedom Fighters. The Thai army started laying into the Freedom Fighters pretty hard, beating them with the butts of their guns and kicking them.

It sounded and looked like they were getting beaten to death, literally, right before our eyes. I could hear bones breaking and muscles tearing. Sweat poured off the Thai soldiers as they unleashed all their pent-up fury on their captives. I had never seen anyone beaten so savagely. I felt sympathy for these guys as I watched them gasping for air and begging for mercy. I had seen enough pain and suffering and death to last me several lifetimes, and I didn't want to witness another minute of it.

As I watched, a deep-seated fear took root in me. For the first time in a long time, I was truly afraid for our lives. The Thai were being extremely cruel, and I feared they might direct their hatred at my brother and me next. Figuring I had nothing to lose, I decided to speak to the guards. I spoke up in Thai and begged them to not hurt us. I told them my mother was old and we were here just to try to buy a bucket so that we could get water and sell it back at camp. I told them all I had was 50 baht to buy the bucket. The Thai asked me if I was Thai. I lied and told them that my mother was Thai and that she gotten stuck on the Cambodian side during World War II.

One of the guards came over to me and pointed an M-16 at my head and told me to lie down. So I lied down on my back, and he put the M-16 right at my forehead. He said, "I am going to search you. If I find any money other than what you told me, I will shoot you in half." While he spoke, I prayed frantically to my ancestors to help me. I did not want to die here like this. I did not want my brother to see me die. The guard started to search me, feeling in my waist band, working his way down to my upper legs. He told me to flip over. I did as I was ordered, the hot sun burnt sand stinging my chest and my face. He stuck the gun in my back and continued his search. My panic grew as he made his way down toward my feet. He made it as far as my calves. For some reason, he stopped. He never found the money. He told me to sit up, I continued watching the beating of the Freedom Fighters again.

I was getting increasingly afraid for my life. My efforts to find favor with the Thais had failed, and I wasn't sure what else I could do. All sorts of things started going through my head.

Would it be better to be shot and killed than beaten like that? (I decided I'd rather have a bullet in the head). Then suddenly, out of nowhere, they let me go!

I ran all the way back to camp. I don't think I had ever run so fast in my life. I did not dare look back because I was afraid that they were going to just shoot me in the back, and if that happened, I didn't want to see it coming. While running, it dawned on me I had left my little brother behind. In my fear I had simply run off. How could I do that? I was overwhelmed by guilt and could only figure that my fear and panic had caused me to lose my senses. But there was nothing I could do at that point. It would have been madness to turn back. Fortunately, he caught up with me on my way back to camp. The Thai had searched him, taken his money and let him go. My prayer to my ancestors had worked. I figured it would be some time before I did another run across the border.

Several weeks later, our money was once again running low and I knew I had to head out again. After the last trip I did not want to endanger anyone else's life so I took this trip alone. I gathered up the money and left the camp. I made my way to a village on the Thai side and bought a 25-pound bag of eggplant. On the way back, we ran into the Bada, a group of revolutionary guards. They were dressed like the US Military, in green boots and camouflage, and were carrying US hardware like M-16s and army-issue .45 caliber handguns. The soldiers gathered us up, sat us all down, and started yelling at us. One of them walked up to me and kicked me so hard in the face with the toe of his boot that it just about knocked me out. I felt dizzy and had a hard time gathering my thoughts after that. The guard warned us not to leave the camp area again, threatening to kill us if we did. After the stern warning he told us all to leave. We cleared out of there in seconds and I headed back to camp with my bag of eggplant, and found my family. By trading the eggplant for other staples, we managed to keep going for a little longer.

Day in and day out it was the same thing. Go out and look for food to sell or find some sort of way to make money to get food and water. We would go out to the Thai villages or to the flea market and trade or sell what we bought. We bought and sold whatever we could find. Anything to make a little money to buy the things we needed to survive. There was danger involved as well because when you went into the villages you took the risk of getting robbed or shot or killed. We even had to worry about the Thai guards shooting at us. If they saw us crossing the road into the village areas they would use us for target practice with the intent of shooting to kill. One day word spread through camp that the United Nations was going to open a camp in a place called Khao-I-Dang. We held a family meeting to see if anyone was interested in leaving this place and making our way to the new camp. The vote was unanimous. We readied ourselves to leave the camp and started to break down our little area. The day before we left I ran across the old fortune teller who had once told me to head west. He remembered me, so we started talking. I told him I was going to still try and head west. He said he still remembered what he'd told me and that I needed to keep going further west until this place and these times were but a distant memory.

CAMP LIFE

We walked out of Freedom Camp to the main road and when we got there the first thing I saw was this big white man speaking and cursing in perfect Thai. He was madly issuing orders to the Thai Army to help the refugees on the buses that had lined up to take us to Khao-I-Dang. I think there were about 10 buses waiting for us. Our family got on with what little we had and sat down for the ride to Khao-I-Dang.

Khao-I-Dang was a Cambodian refugee camp located 24 kilometers north of the city of Aranyaprathet at the foot of Khao-I-Dang Mountain. The camp was situated on the sparsely wooded plains in the eastern part of the country. The camp covered about 4.8 kilometers which was home to almost 140,000 people when we arrived. We often heard other refugees in camp joke that Khao-I-Dang was the second–largest Cambodian city in the world. The camp was divided into sections, with about 12,000 people in each one. It functioned like a small city, with its own hospital and school. By any measure, it was far better than the last camp we were at. We felt much more comfortable here and were less fearful, as it had less of the daily violence that plagued the Freedom Camp.

Each family had its own small living area. Food and fresh water were delivered daily, and we received a regular allocation of rice, canned fish, beans, vegetables, and cooking oil. It felt so good to finally get enough food in our bellies every day. For so many of us, it had been so long since we had enjoyed any satisfaction at the end of a meal. After four years of eating food with no seasoning, it was amazing to enjoy sauces and flavoring again. A little soy sauce here, some fish sauce there, a sprinkling of ginger—as a cook, I reveled in the simplest tastes and thought they were gifts from the gods. We were each responsible for cooking our own food and for finding the wood to cook with. Traveling in pairs for safety, we scrambled up into the hills every day to gather wood. Most in the camp had to survive on what was given to them. If you wanted anything beyond the absolute basics—clothes, extra food for your family—you had to have money. So if you knew how to hustle and make money, you were a little better off. Through my trading, I had been able to stash away about 2000 baht (about 100 dollars), which helped us get what we needed.

At one point, the Thai split up the camps and moved the Chinese all the way down to the end of the camp. We all built little shacks out of blue tarp, bamboo, and whatever else we could scrounge up. Each family had its own small shack, which gave us modest Chinese at least a small sense of privacy. Our family unit consisted of Kim, my mother, Chai, my mother-in-law, Kim's seven little brothers and sisters, my sister and her son, and a family friend and her three children. This meant there were 20 people living in a space of about 20 feet by 12 feet. At night we lined everyone up next to each other and dropped the mosquito net down onto everyone. You had to be extra careful not to roll over in the night because you would wake up everyone in the line!

Camp life was a mixed blessing. There were patrols inside the camp every night and they were serious about keeping people in their sections. We had a 7 p.m. curfew, after which we were expected to stay in our sections until sunrise. There was a guard tower on every corner of the camp and the Thai Army patrolled outside the camp. There were times when it felt a bit like a prison. Despite that, morale in camp was on the whole quite good. We felt safer than we had in a long time, and people were eating daily. It is amazing what regular food can do to satiate people. I learned that there were ways around the rules—sympathetic guards who could be bribed to let us out of camp so that we could buy groceries at the nearby village, and so on.

During this time, two of my brothers elected to return to Cambodia. They were my fourth brother Kheng and third brother Kheang. They were supposedly going to go back to get Kheang's wife, who had stayed in Battambang with her family because she was pregnant. But I sensed they would stay once they'd gotten there, and indeed that is what happened. Kheng found his wife and decided to stay there with her to help her look after her many younger siblings, and Kheang returned to Cambodia because he was in love with someone who had stayed behind. I was dismayed to see them go—I was worried what their life would be like if they stayed in Cambodia—but there was nothing I could do to change their plans.

At the camp, our shack was situated next to a mound of dirt, and my brother-in-law knew the woman who lived on the other side of it. He had his eye on her for a long time, and eventually, he approached her parents and asked for them to arrange the marriage between him and their daughter. The parents agreed. The funny thing about this is the fact my brother-in-law had gone to the same fortune teller as I did. He told him his bride-to-be will be on the other side of the dirt mound from you and that you would get married this year. When my brother-in-law heard those words he thought the old man was crazy. He forgot about what he was told until he was about to be married. Several days before they got married he told me the story and I had to remind him how powerful the fortune teller was.

We were busy getting through each day, getting to know the people around us and trying to make do when the administrators of Khao-I-Dang decided to break everyone up into sections in the camp. I think they did this to help manage the people. We ended up being in section four the whole time we were in camp. Section four had several clinics to help with people's health issues after being neglected under the Khmer Rouge.

While in the camp the U.N. provided doctors to help people with their problems and since many of the workers did not speak Cambodian or even Chinese my mother was able to use her multilingual skills to their fullest. My mother told me to get over there and sign up to be an interpreter as well; I went and signed up and ended up cleaning up around the clinics and acting as a go between for the doctor – patient conversations. The Thai even found Chinese doctors to help the Chinese, but still the Chinese doctors did not speak some of the dialects that came out of Cambodia. I informed the Thai doctors the limits of my Thai and what dialects I could deal with and we made things work. During this time translating Thai to Chinese really helped my Thai as I was able to learn so many technical and clinical words I would not have gotten in daily conversations. Talking with the Cambodians and Chinese was a great experience. I was able to really help people with their health issues and their concerns about camp life, food differences, whatever else was on their minds.

Another major event during this time was Kim's announcement that she was pregnant. I was really worried about the pregnancy. There was still a lot I needed to figure out about our future. We were living in a refugee camp, I was not making any money, and we had nothing to our names. I used to talk to my unborn child and tell the child to wait to come out until we got to America because things would be far better. I really did not want our child to be born in a refugee camp. I told our child I didn't even have enough money for diapers. My practical concerns aside, I was extremely excited about the prospect of being a father. For a little while it was hard to wrap my brain around the fact we were having a child. At this point, Kim and I had been married about two months. In that short time, we had left our home country, moved into a camp, and found out we were expecting a baby.

There was no way to tell how long we'd be stuck in the camp. We had no idea when or if we would get a sponsor. Kim and I felt as if we were in a sort of emotional no man's land, stranded between neither here nor there. I went and talked with the camp administrators and gave them any information they asked for. In the back of my mind I was still heeding the fortune teller's words on my life to go as far west as I could so I requested the U.S.A. as my first choice of a country to end up in. I was asked about my family members and if I had ever been in jail. I told them I had been in a hell called the Khmer Rouge in Cambodia and was happy to be out of there.

Money was getting tight again so I was forced to make another trip out of camp to get some money for the family. After all my successful trading and border crossing, my luck finally started to run out. One time when we snuck out of the camp, I was able to get a hold of 20 pineapples, and my brother-in-law grabbed all the toilet paper he could afford to buy. When we returned to camp, the guard who had let us out was no longer there. So they started shooting at us from the guard tower. Now, just inside the fence, was a ditch we had to jump across to get back to our place. I made it across with my pineapples, but my brother-in-law and his load of toilet paper didn't. We were so afraid that night we did not even think about going back for the toilet paper. It was a valuable commodity in camp, but we just left it sitting right where it fell.

The next time family members made a trip out of the camp, I had to be talked into going. I was nervous after the last trip. But I went anyway. We made it to the village without incident, only to discover there was nothing to buy. We returned to camp, and the soldiers opened fire on us again. This time, we were all rounded up by the camp police and taken away to their little jail. I quickly wrapped up what money I had and stuck it in my boxer shorts so I could tell the police I'd lost my money on the way back from the village. They ended up keeping us there for three miserable days. I was worried that they might decide to torture us, but they just made us run laps around the camp. I was angry at being locked up for going to a village—freedoms that other people in the world enjoyed every day—and angry because all I was trying to do was provide for my family. But they eventually released us without further trouble.

When I got out of the camp prison I confidently told my family I would be on a ship leaving to America in one month. I said to them, "One month and no more of sneaking out of camp to get food. One month and no longer sleeping on the ground and living in a stinking camp surrounded by hundreds of thousands of people". I knew I was going to make it out of this place and soon. I do not know how I knew, but I just felt something was coming up for me. In the back of my mind, I was still thinking of what the fortune teller told me. It became like a mantra, the further west I go, and the better my life will be.

BETWEEN KHAO-I-DANG
AND AMERICA

Little did I know that one month later I would receive the name of someone willing to sponsor my wife and me. Only one month after making that promise to myself, my neighbor came over and said to me, "Hey I saw your name up on the list. You have a name that will get you to America!" I did not believe him and told him to stop teasing me about something so important. Just in case he was telling the truth, I headed over to the office where they posted names. I forced my eyes up to the names board, my heart beating rapidly in anticipation, and what I saw made me jump and scream with happiness. Our names were there and we were on our way! I ran back to our little area and told Kim of the good news. Her eyes sparkled brightly when she listened to what I told her. She knew our unborn child was going to be blessed by being born in a new country. This also meant that we could join my brother Heng in the States.

You see, my brother Heng had made it across the Thai border back in 1979 and made his way to a monastery where he heard the Red Cross was helping people with getting out of Thailand. One day, while everyone was sitting around the Red Cross started calling out names of people from a list and my brother heard someone calling his name. Several times he heard "Kok Heng, Kok Heng". My brother looked around and, realizing no one had claimed the name raised his hand. The Red Cross representative told him to get on the bus and the next thing he knew, he was in Seattle. Heng could not believe his luck. To this day, he does not know whether the Kok Heng the Red Cross was calling for was even him. But he saw his chance and took it. As soon as Heng arrived in Seattle he started mailing letters to our camp hoping the letters would reach us. Somehow the letters arrived and landed on the desk of a person who I had been working with. He looked at the letters, came and found me and told me that someone named Kok Heng was sending me letters from Seattle. When we were in camp my little brother had been working hard to get us sponsored, and not much later, our names appeared on the leave list at Khao-I-Dang.

The problem that was facing me now was that our paperwork was for me and my wife only and not for anyone else in our family. How was I going to break this to the rest of the family? I had worked hard to keep the family together, and without me who would be the new family leader? I gathered everyone together and told them as soon as I got to where I was going, I would start the sponsorship process to bring them to the United States. I asked them to be strong and take care of each other and soon we would be together as a family. They were happy one of us was leaving the camp and that I would forge the path for them to follow. They knew I would not forget about them and I would get to work on their behalf as soon as I got to wherever I was going. After making sure the family was going to be fine without me, I got practical and started to work on learning a new language.

I went immediately to find one of my cousins' who spoke not only the languages we spoke but English and French as well. I asked him to please teach me some beginning English skills because I was going to need to be able to speak at least some English when I get to the United States. While studying we found out we were going to have other worries as well. Early in 1980 (when I got my notice) they split Khao-I-Dang and sent some of the refugees further away from the border. This was because the Khmer Rouge were still fighting hard. There were many factions that were actively involved in continuing the war in Cambodia. The Khmer Rouge were fighting the Vietnamese and attacking the Thai Army at the Thai border. There were several instances of mortar rockets landing in Khao-I-Dang with people dying from explosions. There were rumors floating around camp from people who had family members been beaten, robbed, tortured and even killed in border excursions from the Khmer Rouge. This only made things in camp much tenser. There was now an edge of nervousness to the camp. I likened the camp to being a bunch of chickens waiting to be fattened up for the slaughter. Sometimes the camp felt like jail. All of us penned in together behind a fence waiting for the bombs to drop or the Khmer Rouge to make it to the camp and start wholesale slaughter.

For some reason the camp administrators changed things drastically. They segregated people at the camp according to what race of people you belonged to. So the Chinese stayed with Chinese, Vietnamese with Vietnamese, Laotian with Laotian. I never found out why they did this. It could have been grouping people like that made it easier when they shipped out groups of people? Maybe certain countries were only taking limited numbers of certain ethnic groups? I do not know. What this meant for my family is they had to move to the Chinese camp. We had made friends while in camp and this would once again uproot us from a situation we had started to feel comfortable in. There was no time to be sad or contemplate anything else because once the decision was made and announced to the camp across the loud speakers people ran to the post office bulletin board to see where they would be moving. That meant we had to break down our little place, gather everything up and get on a truck and move. No saying goodbye to those around us, just get it done in a hurry.

Around this time I came across my cousin's wife from Phnom Penh; her husband's father is my mom's second oldest brother, and while talking with her I found out my uncle's whole family had died. There were fifteen people in the family that disappeared. She told me the uncle and the aunt starved to death and the rest the Khmer Rouge killed off because someone in the Khmer Rouge hierarchy got wind my cousin's family was educated and the educated were the first to go. A truck came by the camp where the family was staying at and took the whole family away. No one knows where the family was killed at or what happened to the bodies. I can only assume they were killed and buried in a mass grave somewhere.

She was so full of grief she could do nothing but cry and was always threatening to take her own life. I didn't know what to do for her. Here I am again, dealing with the remnants of the Khmer Rouge. I was thinking no matter how hard I tried to put the pain and suffering of the Khmer Rouge years behind me, they always seemed to come back to haunt me in new ways. I asked myself a number of times "Would the pain in my heart ever end?" I thought about my cousin's pain and endless grief for several days and realized that I had a schedule to meet of my own and if I did not pull it together I was going to miss my own interview to get out of this place. I hustled over to the office and started my interview. I had heard around camp if the interview went well, you were on your way. I had no idea what to expect. What if they wanted to do the interview in a language I did not understand? What if they wanted me to speak English? I was very nervous. On the day of the interview, I went to the office, sat down and waited several hours until my name was called. As I entered the office, I prayed to my grandmother for help. The fellow who gave the interview asked me what language I wanted to use and we spoke Chinese to each other. They asked me who was sponsoring me in the U.S.A. and what their relationship was to me and how many more family members I had in camp. That was it. As I left, I thought to myself, "I scared myself to the point of passing out and that was it?"

The interview must have gone well because I was told in two days time we would board a bus to a place called Phanat Nikhom Refugee camp, situated in the Chonburi Province southeast of Bangkok. Two days later, we headed off to the bus. As we were getting our meager belongings ready my wife became extremely emotional about leaving her family. Kim and her mother's tears were a mix of sadness and joy—sadness at leaving one another, but joy at the prospect of a future beyond the camp. There were many people crying as we boarded the bus. We stepped up the stairs of the bus and turned around and took one last look back at our family. We peered deep into their faces as if to memorize them, worried this might be the last time we ever saw them.

A few hours later, we arrived at a temporary camp. There were Cambodian, Lao and Vietnamese refugees there. The camp was separated from the outside world by a barbed wire fence, through which no one could enter without proper documentation. There were armed security personnel at the gates and wooden guard towers. Under Thai law, we were now considered illegal aliens. The camp was its own foreign land, with street names like California Street, Texas Road, and New York Avenue. Although it was an ugly, prison-like place, we didn't really care. Being here meant we would soon be headed toward freedom. For the first time, the prospect of being free felt real, and I finally let myself believe it would really happen. I spent time the first day trying to imagine what America would look like, what the food would taste like. Would the air be different? Would the sun be warm like it is here?

There was little time for daydreaming. We needed to get situated in our new temporary living quarters. We were assigned to a brand new building that did not have dirt floors. For this we were happy. We ended up sharing our space with a family of six in a room that was about sixteen by 20 feet. By any measure, this was much better than the previous camp, but we hardly noticed. We were focused on the future at that point.

The next day, I went to see if my name had been posted on the bulletin board. It wasn't there, which frightened me. I thought someone had played a trick on me or maybe our paperwork had fallen apart or the sponsor had changed their mind. I turned to my wife and spoke to my unborn baby and asked her to please wait to be born until we got to America. Kim was about 7 or 8 months pregnant by this time and we were really getting nervous that our child would want to come out early. I felt helpless as there was no way to make any money here. We just had to sit around and wait. Sitting around and waiting is not my style. I like to be able to make moves and work and make money so I can improve my situation. I was restless and impatient.

After several days of looking for my name on the wall I was feeling we may get stuck here indefinitely in this no-mans land. Finally I saw my name up on the wall! That meant that we would soon be on our way. The same day I went and set up an appointment to get an exit interview. At the appointed time, I went and interviewed with a young embassy employee, who spoke a little Thai. The first question he asked was if I spoke any Thai. I told him that I speak a little Thai and so we did the interview in that language. The next question he asked me was if I had ever been in jail. He didn't realize he had asked me a rather complicated question. I calmly told him that I had been in a jail with no walls, no guards, and no fence. That jail was called hell. I told him I left one section because I was hungry and I heard another section had plenty of food to eat, so I left to go to the other section. The Khmer Rouge captured me and tortured me until I acted crazy and they let me go.

The next question after that was, "What is your religion?" A lot of people in the camp had started to go to church, mainly because there was a rumor floating around if you were not Christian, you would not make it to America. I was thinking of saying Buddhist but I did not think they would like me if I said I was Buddhist. I also heard another rumor if you lied during the interview and they found out you lied, they would hold you in camp for as long as they wanted. So I told them I upheld the family belief, which was ancestor worship (I prayed to my deceased relatives for guidance and strength). The fellow said, "Hmmm. Ok. That is a ghost religion."

After those two questions, he smiled at me, looked down at his desk, took a pen slowly out of its holder, and signed a piece of paper. He then stood up from behind his desk, stuck out his hand for me to shake and told me, "Well, good luck." That was it. I was then told in two days we had to go to the INS for a medical check up. I went back to our little place and slept well for the first time in a long time. Two days later, we went to the medical office for our visit. An enormous man greeted me. We had heard that he was mean and that if you did not answer the questions correctly, he would not sign the paper and you wouldn't get to see him again for a long time. He started to ask me the same questions the last fellow had asked me, which I thought was kind of strange. But it seems that I answered fine. We then got tested for Tuberculosis, cholera and malaria, and they asked me about the health of my wife. I told them that she was pregnant but I was not sure how far along she was in her pregnancy. I was told the interview was over and I should go back to my living area and wait to see what was going to happen next.

We spent a total of eleven days in Chonburi and were finally released to another final camp called Buriram. We had to wait three days at the transfer camp for the charter plane to show up. We were trying not to be impatient, but we had been in transit for a long time by now and were very ready to leave. America was no longer a distant dream but a concrete reality we had to be ready for. Part of me was ready for this new adventure, and part of me was scared to death. The night before we left someone stole a piece of my luggage that was very important to Kim and me. What little money we had was in there and I knew that we were going to need some money. I called up my uncle and told him about our plight. He sent his chauffeur to the camp with 2000 baht (back then about 100 dollars or so).

Our picture taken at Chonburi before we left

We got on the bus to go to the airport in the middle of the night. The bus took us to a military base. It took a long time to get everyone sorted out, but eventually, I was sitting next to my wife on the plane. Because I helped the Thai converse and coordinate with the other refugees, Kim and I were able to sit in first class all the way. From Bangkok, we flew to Hong Kong, where the plane refueled. I could barely contain my excitement. Here we were on our way, finally leaving the chaos that Cambodia had become behind us. Sitting on the plane in the tarmac, it seemed like all of the insanity was already a lifetime ago. After Hong Kong, we flew to Alaska for another refueling. As we landed, the pilot told us over the intercom that we were landing in America. You should have heard the people on the plane yelling with joy, everyone screaming the same thing: "We have a second chance at life!" and "We are finally free!"

From Alaska, we flew to San Francisco. We were let off of the plane and taken over to the Presidio. While we filled out forms, a translator told us, "During this time of the year, it is summer here." All of us were amazed that summer could be so cold. I thought I would never get used to this kind of cold. We spent the night in dormitory rooms in the Presidio. The wind was blowing and a damp fog hung in the air. I had never been so cold in my life and could not stop shaking. We were amazed to see people walking around in shorts and short-sleeved T-shirts. We thought they were crazy. When I lay down in bed that night, a tune I used to hear in Cambodia in the '70's popped into my head: "If You're Going to San Francisco." I used to love the tune back then—it was my favorite song of the time. Amazingly, I had finally made it to San Francisco.

The next day, the INS people told us we were going to fly to Seattle next. This would be the last stop. This would be the place where we would start our new lives. When we got to the airport, I took the 2000 baht I had in Thai money and converted them into American dollars. It came to $96.00 dollars. I went over to get a hot dog. The vendor asked for three dollars. Three dollars for this!? In Thailand I could eat for three days on three dollars. That was a quick lesson for me. I knew my money wouldn't last long if I was not very careful. We caught our plane and were soon landing in our final destination.

SEATTLE AT LAST

When we disembarked, we were greeted by my brother Henry (Heng). With him were our sponsors, Reverend Hicks and his wife, Ruth, who eventually became very good friends. Little did we know then what an amazing couple they were. Ruth Hicks devoted her life to helping refugees, not with money, but in countless other ways—helping people get to the grocery store, teaching them how to shop, finding churches to go to, and so on. Eventually, we became so close to them we always called them Mom and Dad.

We got to their van and Reverend Hicks warned us in America everyone drives really fast. He told us not to get scared when we got on the freeway. And it was true—cars were moving extremely quick, and everything was very loud. That is what really got to me. Everything was loud, too loud for me really. All the noise and speed caused my head to spin a bit.

We got off the freeway near Olive Way and Denny Street and went to meet my mother who had gotten out of Freedom Camp about one month before us. She and my brother Chuck (Chai) shared a very small studio apartment with nothing more than a small kitchen and a bed (the bathroom was out in the hall). The first night, Kim and I slept on the floor. As I lay there next to Kim, I thought, "What am I going to do next?" I had no English skills. I knew I could cook, but I had no idea how I was going to find a job and provide for the baby. It was a long and anxious night.

My family with our sponsors Reverend and Ruth Hicks

We had a hard time sleeping there at the beginning. The city sounds kept us up. Every time we heard a siren, I jumped up out of my sleep with my heart pounding. I would hear someone arguing loudly on the street and it would bring back memories of the Khmer Rouge soldiers yelling at me. It was a lot to adjust to all at once. I was used to hot, humid weather, lush vegetation all around, and quiet. The green of this new place was different from that of Thailand and Cambodia. In the morning the air smelled of a clean clear crispness that took my brain time to get used to. My senses were constantly being thrown off, as they tried to grasp all of this newness. I also realized that I was going to have to get used to dealing with other people who did not look like me, think like me, and speak like me. I was shocked at first that there were so many different colors and shades of people. Some days, it threatened to overwhelm me completely.

I knew it was going to take everything I had to make it here. The good thing was that there were several other Cambodian families down the street and we would hang out with each other and talk about plans for the new life and cook and eat food we knew. Socializing made things a little better for us and made us feel less isolated as we figured out the way this new country worked.

The early days were a blur. We were busy figuring so many things out and getting organized that I can hardly remember it all. We had to go to King County Health and get caught up on our shots. For many years in Cambodia there was no medical care at all, so we had to get our inoculations. We had to go to the Social Security office to sign up to get public assistance until I was able to find work. I had to check into various vocational programs and figure out what I was going to do for a living. I signed up for classes at Seattle Central Community College. We started the process of trying to get Kim's mother and brothers over here, which took a long time as their sponsorship kept getting turned down. The Reverend took us to set up bank accounts, taught us how to cash checks, and showed us how to get around on the bus. I found out about Goodwill and I stocked up on clothes. For those of you who do not know what Goodwill is, it is an organization that takes donations of clothing for sale in their store and the profits help fund job and life skills training for people trying to get back on their feet.

Finally, I knew the time would come soon when I would have to get a job. I knew I was good at hustling and figured that hustling and working hard were the same all over the world. We got by during these early days thanks to donations from our sponsor and his church, who gave us both money and practical items like pots and pans.

One month after getting settled in with my mother, our daughter was born. Our sponsor named her Dawn because she was born at 5:30 a.m. I can remember my wife holding our new baby girl. I saw the love in my wife's eyes and I too fell in love with her immediately. I thought to myself she had to be the most perfect, prettiest baby ever. I picked her up and smelled her skin and put her cheek to mine. She was so soft and smelled so clean and new. My heart swelled with a pride I had never before experienced. I loved Dawn since I laid eyes on her, cuddled up next to my wife. Following Dawn's birth I became so much more loving and compassionate and I had to learn how to drop the defenses that I had built around my heart which enabled me to live through my experiences in Cambodia. How could I look at my beautiful child and not love?

At that exact moment I knew my main responsibility in life would be to provide for my daughter in any way I could. I made up my mind then and there that their lives would never be touched with the horrors I had endured. My mission was to make their lives better than mine. I spent several hours in the room with my wife after she gave birth. Being from Cambodia, I had left my old worn out shoes outside the door. Several hours later, I went to get my shoes and discovered that someone had stolen them! For the life of me, I could not figure out why someone would want to steal my smelly old shoes. I thought to myself: What a funny country. During the Khmer Rouge regime, we left shoes outside all the time and no one ever stole my shoes.

A NEW LIFE:
FAMILY AND WORK

I t finally came time for us to take our new baby home. When we got back to our studio apartment, I realized that my wife had no experience with babies. Since I had grown up in a large family I used to watch relatives with their infants. I knew how to change diapers and give babies a bath. I was proud to be able to help my wife with our child. I bathed her and changed her diapers, and taught my wife at the same time. I used to nap with her on my chest, so I could smell her clean hair. I marveled at how tiny and beautiful she was. We took turns holding her and talking with her really quietly. I also showed my wife how to cook.

I studied English about 3 or 4 hours a day. I had learned so many languages on the fly (Vietnamese, Thai, and so on) that I was surprised at how hard it was to grasp English. After school, I came home and cooked dinner. We shared whatever we made with an older Chinese gentleman who lived in our building. I did this because in our culture, it is traditional for us to look after the older people in our community.

One day when I brought him food, he told me I was a good cook and asked whether I'd like to learn something about cooking American food. I replied I'd like to very much. He worked the evening shift at a restaurant downtown, and he suggested I drop by and watch him sometime. While I was down there, I asked him if he could teach me how to eat. He thought I was crazy at first, but I insisted I needed to know how Americans eat. He let me watch how the plate went out to the customer and I watched the customers through the kitchen door window to see how they ate their food. That's how I learned to make hamburgers and sandwiches and pizza and pancakes and fried chicken.

Man I thought Chinese ate fast, but some of these Americans eat really fast. It looked like they were shoving the food in their face as fast as they could and taking big gulps of water to force the food down their throats. After watching the old man, I became confident I could cook some of these foods. I knew I just had to wait my turn. One day, my friend got sick and the owner who had seen me hanging around, asked me if I could handle the job. I told the owner yes, but I needed the waiters to not write on the ticket because I could not read English yet. I took the menu home that night and translated the menu into Chinese and Cambodian so I could understand what items I was going to be cooking.

I started the next day. On my second day on the job the waitress came into the kitchen and asked for a hamburger deluxe, hold the onion. I thought to myself: hold the onion? How am I supposed to hold the onion? How can I cook and hold an onion? That made no sense to me at all. I asked her what she meant. She smiled and looked at me and said to "just put the onion on the plate, honey." She was a really good person and helped me with American restaurant lingo.

The cooking was going so well I told the owner not to hire a dishwasher during my shift because I could handle both jobs. I worked there for several months, cooking and getting comfortable with using English and making some money to support my family. One day my brother Heng, who was working over at Ivar's Restaurant, called me and told me they needed a bus boy. I hooked up with my brother and we went over to meet the assistant manager. He was from Thailand so I spoke Thai to him. He asked me if I had any experience working in restaurants. I told him I'd grown up in a restaurant family. I told him I would work here for a couple of days and if he did not like my work, he would not have to pay me.

I worked hard for two days to impress the assistant manager and after the two days were up I got the job. He said I'd be working five days a week and making $2.90 an hour. Now I had two jobs. The cooking job was paying me better than the bus boy job, so I was actually making a little bit of money. My days looked like this: I would start my cooking job at 6:00 a.m. I would start by cleaning everything up. I liked to have a spotless kitchen before I start cooking. I washed all the dishes and cut the vegetables for the afternoon cook then headed over to Ivar's Salmon House on Lake Union at 5:00 P.M. I worked there until 11:00 p.m. On the weekends, I did landscaping jobs for people, pulling weeds and mowing lawns, whatever I could do to make money for the family. I was also still going to school when I could. I left the house at 4:30 A.M. and didn't get back until after midnight most nights. I did homework until about 2:00

A.M. before falling fast asleep. And the next day, it would begin again, day after day.

Working as hard as I was I begun to wonder how much of this I could take before I got sick. It turns out I did not take a single day off for the first six years I was in the States. I knew I had to hang on because I had to take care of my wife and daughter. I was so busy working I never had time to think about the past. This helped me bury the pain of the Khmer Rouge deep inside me. There were times when I would have shocking flashbacks— of getting tortured or starving or watching my nephew die right before me. When these memories surfaced out of the depths of my consciousness, I would work even harder at my job. I took a moment or two whenever I could to thank my ancestors for the food we had to eat and a comfortable warm place to sleep. I felt blessed I was able to provide for my wife and child. I even had enough money to send about $50.00 dollars a month back to my mother-in-law's family and I gave money to help my mother as well. When I sat on the bus on the way home from my jobs, I would look out the window and my thoughts would turn to my daughter. What a blessing for her to be born in this country! I wanted for her all the good things this country has to offer.

I proved myself by working extremely hard and soon felt comfortable enough to ask my boss if I could cook. I told them about my cooking experience and they assigned me to do the employee meals. I cooked different types of Asian food for the employees, and sometimes tried to do some American-style dishes to broaden my cooking horizon. I really enjoyed cooking for people and it made me recall my old dream of one day having my own place, and being my own boss like my father had been.

One day at Ivar's they needed a kitchen helper (the person who makes sure the chowders are ready, the meat is cut and ready, food is stocked, and so on). I decided to take the job. It paid a little more and I would get to learn more about working in kitchens in this country.

I worked at Ivar's for three years learning different cooking techniques. I watched and learned how people interacted with each other and I got to use my English every day and the work staff went out of their way to help with my expanding vocabulary. As hard as I was working I was still looking around for work that paid better. As I was leaving Ivar's one day after my shift my little brother Heng came to me and told me of a friend of his who worked at the Rainier Club. Now the Rainier Club is one of the most exclusive clubs in town and for me to get a job there was a move in the right direction. The club has been in existence since 1888 and caters to the Seattle business elite and society crowd. It turns out they were looking for a pantry person. In a professional kitchen the pantry cook is the Sous chef's right hand man. I scheduled a meeting with my brother's friend Lee and the Head Chef Hans on a Friday. The interview went well and was told that I could start in a week or so. I went back to Ivar's, did my shift, and gave my notice.

Our newest addition to the family was born on June 3rd 1983 just ten days after starting at the Rainier Club. The timing of the new job (and the extra money from the raise) was fortuitous. I was going to need the extra money for our growing family. Once again, our sponsor family named our child and she received the name Diane. I now had two beautiful daughters! Things were very tight when the children were first born and we were sleeping on the floor because we could not afford furniture. The Hicks came by to see us and saw how we were living and asked us if we wanted to apply for public housing. I politely told him that I was going to manage the family myself and that I did not want to take advantage of the system because I was working. I remember telling Reverend Hicks "Who knows, maybe one day I will have my own restaurant!"

With two kids, I knew that I was going to have to move out of our studio apartment.We moved to the apartment next door. It was a one bedroom unit with a larger living space. It also meant that Kim and I could have a room of our own. We had no furniture until we went to a flea market. When I heard the word flea market I thought to myself "What a strange country this is! Who in the hell would want to sell fleas? And, even stranger, who in the hell would buy them?"

Work at the Rainier Club was going really well. They started giving me regular overtime hours, which really helped our finances. Even though I was spending a lot of time away from my wife and kids, and working all the time, I had made it out of Cambodia, to America, with a large part of my extended family. I considered myself extremely lucky to be in this position.

The Rainier Club turned out to be a great place to keep on expanding my knowledge of cooking techniques. There were many people in the kitchen who had a great deal of experience and some of the staff had been schooled in different traditions. I asked questions of everyone and absorbed everything I could. When things were slow at work I watched and studied how other people worked. I developed a special interest in fruit carving and started to pursue it in my spare time. I went to stores and looked at how people did fruit trays; studied the photos in books; practiced on fruit at work. After spending many long hours at it, I started to get really good. I could take a radish and make it look like a rose or a watermelon and carve anything I wanted into it. I put my heart into my work, and it showed. Some people just work for a living, but I really tried to learn every day.

Hans and I got along really well and had a good time working together. We used to joke around a lot. When he used to interview people, he would ask me, "Well, what do you think of the guy?" I would answer, "If he walks like me, talks like me, acts like me, hire him because he will be a good one!" He'd let out a huge barrel laugh after that. I'd ask him about his hiring experience and how he knew who was going to be a honest employee. He said he didn't know, so I told him: Comment on his hair, his smell, the way he looks, and his clothes, and if he turns around and calls you an asshole, he is truthful and will be honest and you should be able to trust him. Hans liked that!

There was one co-worker I remember fondly. She was one of their older employees; her name was June Robinson. She was a real character. She worked up in the Cascade room for years. Everytime she came into the kitchen she would start with the trash talking. Mostly what she said was really humorous, bordering on rude really but I liked it and she always laughed at what I said to her; she smoked a lot and had this gravelly voice from years of continuous smoking and the laugh that came out of her was a low rumble. She was not a big woman and when I heard that sound coming from her I never really knew if she was laughing or coughing or both at the same time. Every day she came in after her shift she demanded I make her an ice cream sundae. I would start in with our banter and I tell her the sundae was going to make her fat. She always had something funny to say back to me. Most of what she said was crude and I won't repeat them here but when I remember the things she said they still make me smile to this day.

I had very few days off. But when I did, I made sure I spent it with my kids. I can remember one incident. I decided it was time to take the kids out and do something with them. One of my friends at work was talking about how her kids love to go to Chuck E. Cheese. I asked her, "What in the heck was a Chuck E. Cheese?" She told me what it was and where it was and gave me directions. I gathered up my kids and headed out to the restaurant. We got there and I went up to order a pizza. Even though I had been working on my English my speaking was still not very good. When the lady asked me what kind of pizza I wanted I said, "macaroni pizza please." The lady behind the counter said to me, "We do not have a macaroni pizza." I asked her again, "May I please have a macaroni pizza?" Again she said, "We do not have a macaroni pizza." The lady looked at me strangely and said "Let me get this straight, you want a Macaroni pizza? There is no such thing as a macaroni pizza sir." I pointed to a pizza and said, "What's this?" The lady said to me, "Ahh you want a pepperoni pizza!!" I said, "Yeah gimme that one!" I am sure she went in the back and told the people making it, "I got this dumb ass out here who just ordered macaroni pizza!" At that point what was the difference? How was I supposed to know there was a difference between macaroni and pepperoni?

A GROWING FAMILY

I n June of 1984 our third daughter, Darlene, was born. I sometimes couldn't believe the turn my life had taken: I was this little Cambodian immigrant who suddenly had three American citizens on his hands. My wife and I had hoped for a boy, but when our sponsor, Ruth, told us she had a niece who would gladly adopt a girl, I told her, "Absolutely not. She's my blood, my child. I will love her and raise her as best as I can and try to make the future as bright as I can for her." I remembered how I had loved everything about the U.S. when I was growing up in Cambodia. Now here I was making a life in this country, raising a family, working at a place I liked, doing work I believed in.

Late in 1984, after years of failed attempts to get Kim's mother, brothers and sister here, we finally succeeded. When Kim found out her family was going to arrive soon, she was overcome with emotion. She had not seen them for so long and missed her mother's warm embrace and the advice her mother gave her. Kim had always told me she felt extremely lonely without her family. I know that she really missed and needed to experience them once again. She always told me she feared she would never see her mother and siblings again. When she talked like that I always tried to comfort her, but this was a longing in her heart only her family could fill. Kim was overjoyed when she finally was able to see them. When her family got off the plane there were many emotions that came spilling out of them all. Tears were shed, hugs were given and the time spent apart melted away. The scene at the airport was so touching that people who were walking by were drawn into what they were witnessing, some even moved to tears themselves. Some stopped to ask what the occasion was. I quietly told them my wife's family finally made it out of Thailand and they had not seen each other in about 4 years. They walked away with a smile on their face, content to know they were seeing love in action.

In 1986 I was promoted to Chef de Garde Manger. The Garde Manger position is one of the most demanding in any kitchen where the person must be an expert at many different styles of cooking. I didn't think I had a chance because my English skills were still very limited, but Hans called me into his office and asked me if I wanted it. I told him honestly I thought my English was too limited and I didn't have as much experience as others. Hans told me not worry; I had enough experience for the job. He told me he had been watching me and had been talking to the Sous chef and other workers there and everyone said I was a strong worker, who was dedicated and went above and beyond to do the job. That really brought a smile to my face!

There was a substantial bump in pay on this job and I thought I was really doing well now. One thing I never did while I worked there was I never asked for a raise. Not once. I figured if I worked hard, did what I was asked to do, got along with others, everything would work itself out. In 1987, they called me upstairs to a meeting. I did not know what it was about, but when I walked in, I was told they were going to give me a decent raise because they did not want me to go work anywhere else! I walked back downstairs thinking, "Dang, I pay $275.00 a month for an apartment so with this raise I just about paid for two years rent!" It felt so satisfying to be able to support my family and to be acknowledged for my work ethic.

After they gave me the raise, the general manager would bring me out on the floor during banquets and introduced me to members, telling them I was the one who had done this or that part of the meal. Well, that just made me work even harder for them. I already loved working there. After doing that, they had my complete loyalty.

REACHING MY DREAM

In 1987, I was talking to a friend who had just rented a little spot down in the Seattle Chinatown/International District. He mentioned the space next to his was available and the wheels started turning. It was small and the kitchen would need to be revamped, but I started to get excited. Ever since I had worked in my dad's restaurant as a kid I had wanted to open my own place and I knew this was my chance. I know my father was looking down at me with pride in his heart and a tear in his eye. His son taking after his father getting to run his own business and a restaurant no less just like he would have liked. I thought to myself, what a great place this is, this country, where you can work hard and your dreams can come true.

I decided to take the plunge and go into business for myself. I came up with seven items for the menu all of them different noodle soups like we cooked back home. They would be different from anything else that you could find at that time in the Seattle Chinatown/International District. I did all this in one night, and the menu came gushing forth like a spring of water out of my mind onto the page. The next day I went and talked with the landlord about the cost of renting the space. It would cost $700.00 dollars a month, which I thought was a great deal.

I went and talked with my wife about my plan. She told me it had always been my dream to have a restaurant and since we had been talking and planning on this for years she said to me, "I know you can do this. You are a dreamer and a planner and I know you will work hard to see your dream come true." I called my older brother in California and told him my plans. The very first thing that came out of his mouth was, "Do you have $100,000 dollars? How the hell are you going to start a restaurant without money?" In fact, he wasn't the only naysayer, and I knew all of the statistics of failure for restaurants. I had a vision and knew I could cobble this place together with hard work and cleverness. I knew if I worked hard and offered people something they had not tasted before, I could break through and be a success.

I managed to borrow just enough money—a little here, a little there—to get started, and everything in the restaurant I bought was used except the silverware and the dishes. I tried to get the place running for as little money as possible. Within a month of renting the space, we had it spruced up and looking good and had a menu printed up. By looking at the business from many different angles I had calculated everything down to the smallest detail which allowed me to know what it was going to take for me to make the business a success. While I was cleaning up the place getting it ready for the opening I would notice a few people who would walk by and make comments about my restaurant being too small to be successful. The space I had rented was small but that was ok with me. I knew that starting out small would allow me to slowly build my knowledge of running my own business. I had planned to open the place in the middle of the month so I took a week off from the Rainier

Club and worked night and day (literally) to open the place up. The day before the opening I went shopping for the ingredients I would need to make the special family recipe soup stock. I spent all night prepping things for the opening the next day. I was so excited I did not even need any sleep. I prayed to my dad for good luck, and we opened the doors of the Phnom Penh Noodle house at 8:30 A.M. on July 17, 1987. On Opening day I thought back to my ESL class where my teacher asked me what I wanted to do in the future. I told her that my dream was to open a small café one day. And here I was, on this day with my dream coming true. What made this day even better for me was our place was the first Cambodian restaurant in the city of Seattle.

Phnom Penh Noodle house 1987

My schedule was really grueling because I was still pulling hours at the Rainier Club. After working my shift from 6:00 A.M. to 2:00 P.M. I headed to my place to start cooking all over again. I was working 15 to 16 hours a day, every day, to make things work for my little place. I was rarely home and was often so tired that I fell asleep within seconds of sitting down. I worried I might actually fall asleep standing up! It got so I couldn't even imagine what it would be like to rest anymore. Sometimes I worried how long I could keep up this mad schedule, but there wasn't really any choice. I had to keep it up until the restaurant stabilized.

Things got off to a good start with our little noodle house. Word of our restaurant started to spread and soon we had a loyal clientele for my noodle soups. I enjoyed respect and support from other restaurant owners in the Seattle Chinatown/ International District. People loved the taste of the broth and the combinations of flavors I had created. I was also getting some notice from non-Asian communities and noticed more people from different walks of life started walking into my little place. I got a review in a small Asian newspaper and got even more exposure.

Despite the hard work I had made the right decision in opening up this place. Even though I was still working at the Rainier Club and running my own restaurant I enjoyed what I was doing. I was able to be my own boss when I was at the noodle house and one of the goals I had was to work for myself. Another goal was to work hard when I was young so when I got older things would be easier for my family and me. Unfortunately, the hours I was putting between both jobs finally caught up with me in 1989 when I came down with a bleeding ulcer. I was feeling ill and I thought I just had the flu. Finally things got so bad that I decided to check myself into the emergency room and I am glad that I did. After the doctors looked at me they said that I had only ten percent of my red blood cells left. If I had waited one more day to go to the hospital the doctors said I would have died. They put me into the Intensive Care Unit and gave me a blood transfusion.

The doctors called my wife and she brought our daughter Dawn with her. When they got to my room they were crying because I had all these tubes sticking out of me. I turned to them and said, "It is ok, I will be fine. I am not going to die. I have been through hell and they would not take me so I am not going to die now." Three days later they checked me out with the instructions to not work for a month. Of course I didn't listen to the doctor and went back to work in 10 days. Six weeks later I came back for a follow-up check up with the doctor and he told me that I had a strong immune system and I told him that it was from drinking dead man water while I was in Preah Vihar!!

As my kids got older, I trained them to work in the restaurant as well. Sometimes they complained about working, but I told them this would be the best college that they could ever have. They developed a work ethic I knew would serve them well for the rest of their lives. I knew it had been that way for me. They learned the most important things to me, common sense and street smarts—even more important than a college education. With those two skills, I had been able to guide myself and my family through the hell of the Khmer Rouge and to this great country, train myself to be a great cook, and start my own business. I wanted them to be able to take care of themselves in the same way.

While my family and I were working hard to achieve the American dream of success I started to realize things were not well with my mother's health. She was aging quickly and in and out of the emergency room. We tried to do what we could for her but we knew the end was near. Our family had to make the painful decision to put her in a nursing home. This was very emotional for my mother because she wanted to stay at her apartment. I promised her I would come by and see her every day. I stayed true to the promise that I made to her.

Even though I was working 15 hours or more I made time to check on her. Sometimes she would be asleep and I would leave juice, food, or one of her favorite fruits for her. If she was awake when I came by I would massage her back and talk with her asking her how she felt and if she needed anything. She loved my cooking so I would cook her favorite dish for her. It warmed my heart to see the reaction on her face when I walked in with the food. I would sit there and eat with her and just spend time watching her.

Many times when I showed up my sister was already there with her, holding her hand, talking with her and making sure that my mother was never alone. After recovering at the nursing home my mother was finally able to live on own her again. But things were not stable with her health and she had to return to the hospital. She had been in the hospital for about one week when one Saturday she called me up and asked me to bring her some plain rice soup. She told me she was not feeling well and something was wrong with her. I drove to see her in the hospital and spent a couple of hours with her, just holding her hand. I thought she was going to be ok so I went back to the restaurant. My sister got off work and went to sit with our mother. I got a call from my sister saying that mother does not look good and it may not be long before she dies.

When I got to her room Chai was there with my sister and they both looked worried. I turned and saw her lying there and I knew it was not going to be long. I sat down and held her in my arms and talked with her but the only response was shallow breathing. She stopped breathing while I was holding on to her. Suddenely nurses came running into the room and started to perform CPR on her valiantly working to restart her heart. One of the nurses came out and told my brother, sister and me that our mother had passed away.

We went into her room to say our last goodbyes and as I bent over her I felt relief in my heart because she was finally free from sickness. My mother died May 23, 1992. My brother, sister and I were devasted. Even though we knew it was coming it was very hard to deal with the sudden loss of her. The three of us cried very hard and I could tell my sister was having a hard time. I told her it was ok because now our mother was free from suffering. I went to our mother's bedside and I took hold of her hand and said to her, "It was ok to go, do not worry about us, rest in peace, Dad is waiting for you." I had a hard time trying to get through saying that to her because I knew the words coming from me were going to be some of the last I was going to say to her. We buried her in Lakeview Cemetery in Seattle, Washington. When they were burying her the last thing I said was "In the next life please accept me to be your son again." On the tombstone is a picture of her and my dad on a metal plate so they are together once again.

I buried my grief inside of me and went back to working the restaurant and trying to be the best father I could be and I took pleasure in having the girls working at the restaurant. It reminded me of my family back in Cambodia before the arrival of the Khmer Rouge. Sometimes, though, those memories brought back memories I didn't want to recall. I'd experience flashes of pain and torture. I would get so angry I feared I would snap like a stretched rubber band. At times, the pressure of trying to keep those memories from taking over my life threatened to overwhelm me completely. I held on as best I could because the task of making our life in the U.S. work was up to me. One thing I did make time for in my busy schedule was to take our girls on vacation every year after the school year was over. We took them to Disneyland, to Las Vegas and to Long Beach, California to see my brother and their cousins.

Although my life was far from Cambodia, my past still haunted me. Sometimes I would wake up in a sweat from dreams of torture so real it felt like I was there again, in that room, hanging from my wrists, being beaten. I tried to fight the dreams, but I soon realized it was better to let them come and wash over me so I could somehow cleanse my soul by releasing what was trapped inside my consciousness. I was looking for some sort of release from the dreams and the past. I am not a drinker so I could not hide in a bottle. I worked hard every day to exhaust myself to not dream. For the first fifteen years after coming to this country, the dreams came almost nightly.

I can only assume there were others with the same past, suffering quietly, and hiding behind the mask of reality. The dream that haunted me was dark, filled full of smoke with houses burning, people suffering, the agony and the stench of death all around. I saw relatives who had died, standing in a line as if they were waiting to go somewhere. I would walk up to them and ask them where they were going. No matter which of them I asked, the reaction was the same, a blank stare, nothing ever coming out of their mouths. It felt so real that whenever I awoke from this dream I looked over at my sleeping wife to make sure I was still here. In another dream, I was caught in the crossfire of bullets, and the only thing I could do was to jump into a ditch and hide. I could hear and feel the bullets hitting the dirt around me, the sound of the bullets whistling past my head. I told some of the older people about these dreams. Their advice was to not talk to the dead in my dreams, because if they answer you, it means that you are going with them. Meaning I would die in my dreams and die in real life at the same time. As time passed, the dreams visited less frequently and the razor-sharp edge of those memories dulled a bit. As the impact of the dreams gradually faded, I began to enjoy a new sense of calm.

In 1993, while working at the Rainier Club they hosted the Asia-Pacific Economic Cooperation meeting that President Clinton would be attending. I grabbed one of my business cards with my name on it and asked the elevator operater if she could get the President to sign it. She asked him and his reply was "I don't sign my name for just anyone you know." She told him I was the chef who prepared his lunch. We all know he loved to eat so he signed the card. I am extremely proud of that signature! This got me thinking really hard. How many refugees did I know that came to this country and were able to feed the most powerful man in the world but also get his signature and thanks for feeding him? ME!

There were many highlights during my years at the Rainier Club. I got to meet both President Clinton and Vice-President Gore. I became a senior member of the kitchen staff and enjoyed the respect and camaraderie of the other employees. I worked and learned and trained others. But in 1995, after 13 years, I finally realized it was time to move on and devote my attentions fully to my restaurant. I left the Rainier Club and continued to develop my own business and fruit art skills. In 1996, the Business Improvement Association asked me to present my fruit cutting skills at the Seattle Chinatown/International District festival and I have been presenting my fruit art every year since. I get a real kick out of people when they come by and comment on my vegetable flowers and fruit carving. They always ask me what school I went to learn this skill and I tell them that I learned from looking in a book and watching others around me. People would tell me, "Oh, you have a gift!" I would tell them it was practice and my will that allowed me to develop the skill.

Sadly, on February 10th 1997, the roof of the building where our restaurant was located came crashing down. There had been a huge snow storm in Seattle and snow had accumulated on the roof. After several months of haggling, I signed the lease on a new—much bigger—place. I updated the menu, developed a slew of new recipes, and expanded the menu from seven noodle soups to over 38 dishes.

I wanted to make the new restaurant look more like Cambodia. I bought bamboo and cut it to look like a Cambodian hut, built a fountain at the entrance of the restaurant, added an aquarium, and spruced the place up with new décor. We opened six months after closing the old place. We were delighted when so many people showed up to express their support and friendship in helping us celebrate. We had the customary lion dance for good luck. With a bigger kitchen I was able to do more catering and I became involved in more community events. I donated my time and catering services to the CARE organization. I helped fellow Cambodians with fund-raising parties at my restaurant. Now, 14 years after opening at this location, I am proud to say we are a well-established part of the community. When I was a teenager back in Cambodia I imagined I'd one day be the owner of my own business, continuing my father's legacy with my children working by my side like I had with my father. I found it amazing that in this land of dreams I had realized mine. Along the way my children grew up in our culture and learned to speak our dialect, TeoChew, and Cambodian as well.

Sam is not only a great chef but a master fruit carver as well

RETURNING TO CAMBODIA

Although the topic came up from time to time, my brothers and I did not think about returning to Cambodia for a long time. The country was still in political turmoil, and we had heard over and over again from other Cambodians who had made the trip: "It is best not to return just yet. Wait until things get better." I stayed in touch with my brothers over there, but I missed them greatly. I wanted to see them and hug them. I wanted to sit down with them and enjoy a cup of coffee just like we did when we were younger. Although I managed to talk with my brothers from time to time, I really wanted to see them in person.

Finally, in 2001, we made the trip. My brother Kheng was moving into a new house in Sisophon, and my brother Kheang's daughter was getting married in Battambang. We all felt it was a good time to go back. My brothers Chuck (Chai), Henry (Heng), Tony (Tong Meng) and I all decided to make the trip together. We had not seen our brothers in Cambodia since we had left 21 years ago, which was a long time, especially for a family that was as close as ours was. During our time apart, my brothers in Cambodia had families of their own and started successful businesses. We knew there was a lot for us to catch up on but I will tell you this my brothers and I in the U.S. were extremely apprehensive about going back to a place where we had experienced so much pain and anguish.

From left to right: Chai, Kheng, Me, Tong Meng, Kheang, Heng

We flew to Bangkok, where we met up with my cousin Hon (John) from Hong Kong (whom we had not seen since his family fled Cambodia in 1975), my deceased brother's daughter and fiancé, his son and widow from Australia. There were a total of ten of us in Bangkok. Once we were all there, we boarded a van and made the trip down to the Thai/Cambodian border.

As the vans got approached the border, I could see the outline of my third brother up ahead in the distance. As we got closer, I started to cry so hard it scared me. I have never cried that hard in my life. We all piled out of the van on the Thai side of the border, where my brother and his family were waiting for us. I gave each of my brothers a huge embrace. We started to walk across the border and I spotted a sign off to my left on which was written, "Welcome to Cambodia." I looked at the sign and it made me cry even harder. It finally dawned on me I was really home. I had tried for so long to distance myself from the memories of my country, but it held such a special place in my soul. I leaned toward my brothers and put my arm around them. The more I touched them, the more the tears flowed. A flood gate had opened and it felt good. In fact, I started to feel lighter. It was only then I fully realized how much I had missed the physical presence of my family.

Twenty-one years is a great distance to traverse in the first meeting. As I stood there, I felt the distance dissolve with my tears and put my arms around all of the family I could get a hold of. I had not known what to expect, but I felt in my heart I was home again, truly home, and ready to see how Cambodia had changed since we left.

Once we crossed into Cambodia, we walked around the border village of Poipet for a little while. I immediately noticed the motorcycles. When we left Cambodia, there were only two ways to get around— on foot or by ox cart--and only the Khmer Rouge had motorcycles. But now, it seemed everyone was zipping around on motorcycles. People had more disposable money and could finally afford something as lavish as a motorcycle.

Next, we went to Sisophon to see my brother Kheng's new house. He had started a business selling motorcycle parts and had done extremely well for himself. It filled my heart with pride to see him so successful. We had a big family gathering there with food and drinks. Everyone was so happy that day. To see all of those smiling faces and the joy of laughter warmed my heart.

It made Cambodia seem like home again. We ate and partied and shared memories with each other late into the night. The next day, we headed to Battambang for my niece's wedding. My brother in Battambang, Kheang, was also in the motorcycle parts business and had done extremely well for himself.

The wedding followed traditional Cambodian customs. The bride and groom dressed up in traditional attire and greeted all of their guests by bowing to them. The bowing and the raising of the hand symbolize many things in our culture. People use their hands in prayer or to beg for money. While the Khmer Rouge was in power, we used to raise our hands and beg for mercy. For the bride and groom, the raised hands were a gesture of thanks to the guests for coming to their wedding. Another custom is to give out little bits of money to important guests as a way of saying thanks. When all the guests are seated the official ceremony takes place. It is a beautiful ritual, which ends with the bride symbolically washing the groom's feet.

Everyone was in festive spirits when we returned to my Kheang's house. We ate and drank coffee and sat on the front stoop and talked for hours. Other family members would come out periodically to see how we were doing and realized we were happy right where we were. Sometimes, we just enjoyed the silence. The lack of words created a space no one felt any need to fill up. It felt so good to be still and calm and not rushing or worrying about anything or anyone, but just savoring this unique moment in time. All of my nieces and nephews that I did not know came out of the house and hugged us. They cried and told us that we are all of one blood and one family and thanked us for coming to meet and visit with them. It was a very emotional time and there were so many people to get to know in Battambang and Sisophon.

After the wedding parties were over, we moved our family gathering back to Sisophon for the house-warming party for my brother's new home. Every day while we were in his house, there was a caterer cooking for us all day long. My brother told his wife to grab an employee and go to the public market and buy the best of what he could find in the market that day: the biggest shrimp, the best jackfruit or durian, the best cut of beef or pork. He spared no expense. He would sit at the table with a huge smile on his face while we ate like there was no tomorrow. After we were done eating, we would share some laughs, relax for a while, and start in on dessert. There was so much camaraderie amongst us and a profound feeling of satisfaction for this precious moment in time, we were family again, and the years apart had been wiped away. Later that night before we retired for the night my brother Kheng came to us and said, "For the past twenty one years I felt like I was an orphan, today, I have my family together again. I have a feeling of being whole once more. This is the best day of my life, having my brothers here with me again, to celebrate our new house. I will treasure this day as long as I live."

Once the house warming party wrapped up, it was time for us to leave. It was a bittersweet moment. It was extremely difficult to let go of the family we had reunited with, especially after bonding over the last two weeks. In such a short time, we had become close to so many nieces and nephews, uncles and aunts. My heart was torn in two. I was surprised to realize I would have been perfectly happy not to leave at all.

I knew I needed to return to my children, my wife, my restaurant, and my community obligations. But I vowed right then and there to come back as much as I could. I knew we were all getting older and I wanted to be able to see my brothers as much as I could. Although I have not made it back every single year, I have been back several times, and each trip was better than the last. On one of my trips, I brought my two youngest daughters and my sister over to meet their family. This was my sister's first trip back after twenty five years in the U.S. What really amazed me the most was the immediate bonding of my daughters and their cousins. Even though they had never met they quickly became inseparable. It warmed my heart to see them speak Cambodian with their cousins and family and have them fall in like they were old friends. It reminded me that the most important thing in my life, no matter where we live, no matter what happened in the past, is our family ties.

OLD FRIENDS

I have been fortunate in that I have run into some of the people that were in my life during the Khmer Rouge time. I find it amazing that we were able to connect with each other after so many years. I was looking in particular for two people that had played a part in my past. One was Hong. From time to time thoughts of her entered my consciousness and I would say a little prayer hoping that she had made it out of Cambodia. One of my regular customers knew a fellow in the Bellevue, Washington area who knew Hong's oldest brother. I called him and we talked about our lives back and then and he asked me if I wanted to call Hong and talk with her. She is living in Ottawa Canada, is happily married, has one son and is content with her life. I sent her a letter with my family picture, told her about what I had done with my life and that I too was happily married, had three daughters and owned a restaurant. I had an aunt that lived in Ottawa for years and when she passed away I went up for the funeral. I made a point to go see Hong and to meet her family. It was very nice to see her after 23 years. I am glad that she was able to make it to Canada and has a good life. Since I had made contact with Hong there was one other person I knew I had to find.

There was one incident that was ever present in my dreams. I was out with a friend of mine, foraging for food when we came across two Khmer Rouge soldiers. No matter how hard I tried I could not remember his name. I could see his face but that was it. Nothing else came to mind. I thought of him for years only as the mystery man. I was in my restaurant on October 8 2009, when a long time customer of mine brought his in-law from Massachusetts. I was walking out of my kitchen and saw someone at a table staring at me intently. He looked me up and down several times and I was thinking, "What the hell is wrong with this person??" As I walked past the table he stood up and asked me, "Are you Seng?" "Are you Seng?" Everytime he asked I shook my head yes. He said "Remember me from Anlong Run 1979? We were out looking for food and we got shot at by the two Khmer Rouge soldiers? And you turned around and pulled out your machete and tried to run into the Khmer Rouge? Do you remember that?" My response was, "Oh yeah I remember now! For years I had forgotten who was with me! That was you! You were my mystery man!" The funny thing is the night before he came to my restaurant he was talking with his brother-in-law about me and said he had been looking for me for thirty years! He had been looking in every state that had a large Cambodian population. We made a pact with each other that day to always stay in touch with each other. I have called him several times to talk about the old days and to just say hi. I was so glad to see him alive and doing well.

Bong Cin visit in Seattle

EPILOGUE:

I would like to thank my parents and my teachers who made me what I am today. They took the time to teach me common sense and instilled in me my value system of being kind to others and helping those in need.

I wanted to take a portion of the book to tell others what I think are important values for living a good life. I feel this is important because when we get to the end of our lives, we must realize we will be judged not only by what we did for our families but how we were able to help other people's lives as well.

In life we all have dreams. I say: Don't just dream the dream. Search for it and live and work for the dream. We all have to pay the price to get what we want and to be what we want. No matter what happens always be true to yourself. I was told by my parents to not expect anything more than what you have and to not look up too high, keep your eyes looking straight ahead. This means that you have to focus on what you want. If you keep looking ahead, you can work towards what you want. I believe it is very important to not forget where you came from and to always have a humble heart.

Always put your heart and soul into what you do and you will succeed. Remember we all make choices in this life, sometimes good, sometimes bad. No matter the outcome of your decision, never give up. Try to learn from your mistakes. That is what allowed me to get out of Cambodia alive. If someone criticizes you, they must have a reason for saying what they are saying. Listen to it and learn from what they are trying to tell you. Work on your common sense, which should be based on asking questions using who, what, when, where, why and how. If you do that, then you can find the solution to many of life's problems. If you fail at something, ask yourself how you could do it better the next time around. Keep an open mind. Whenever I do something I always ask myself how can I do it better.

We have to remember we are all human and everyone on this planet needs each other and we are all connected to each other. We are all here doing what we are doing. Sometimes mistakes are made. We need to learn to forgive each other. Along with forgiving, we have to learn how to respect others.

A true friend is someone who helps you when you are down and will lift you up and help you out even when things are really bad. They will always be there for you when there are laughs to be shared and when there are tears to be shed. This is someone you can count on.

I never really had too much of an education in this life and I've really never read a book from cover to cover, but I never let that stop me from learning. I used my skills with languages to learn three Chinese dialects (TeoChew, Cantonese and

Mandarin). I can also speak Cambodian, Thai, Vietnamese and English. This taught me I can learn from those around me. I keep my ears open, and I learn from listening and watching others carefully.

In the end, I can say I am not a perfect human being. None of us are. But I just try to do the best I can with what I know. We need to care for each other; we need to look after our neighbors and friends and develop the bond of community so that, in the end, we do what we can to make the world a better place for all of us.

WRITERS'S NOTES:

S am and I have known each other for about 15 years and has always been telling me little parts of his stories. Sometimes I would come into his restaurant and he would tell me about some dream he had and I began to realize he was still suffering from what had happened to him under the Khmer Rouge. Finally, after years of joking with each other, he asked me to help him write his life story. We got together every Wednesday for almost two years without fail and recorded his stories. There were times when I walked out of there stunned by what he and his family had been through. I knew from my light reading on the subject that things during the Khmer Rouge were difficult, but his stories shook me to my core. I often thought "How can people be that cruel to each other?"

I consider Sam asking me to help him write this book one of the highest honors of my life. When we undertook this venture, Sam said to me it was his wish that writing this book would change my life. I can tell you it certainly has. Being able to take a trip to Cambodia and see people who accept what they have and are at peace with that has made me realize how spoiled so many of us are in this country. Writing this book has made me more thankful and grateful for the people and love that surround me.

*Christine Gregoire: Governor of
Washington State*

Al Gore

*Gift from Former President
Bill Clinton*

Letter from Al Gore

*Gary Locke: Governor of Washington state
from 1997 To 2005: Former United States
Secretary of Commerce*

*James Donald: CEO Starbucks
from 2005 to 2008*

Hem Heng: Ambassador
Of Cambodia to U.S.

H.E. Norak Ratanak: Secretary of State
Kingdom Cambodia

Dawn, Diane, Sam, Kim, Darlene

From left to right: Derin, Dawn,
Damon and Devin